On the Road

Twenty Great Day Trips from McCall

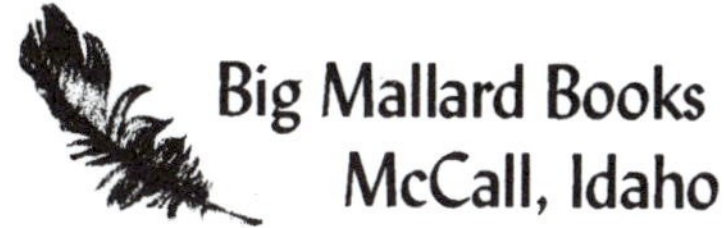

On the Road

Twenty Great Day Trips from McCall

Kathy Deinhardt Hill

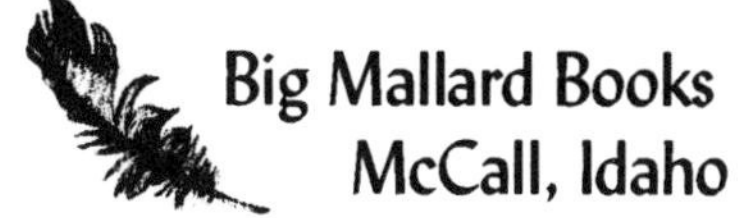

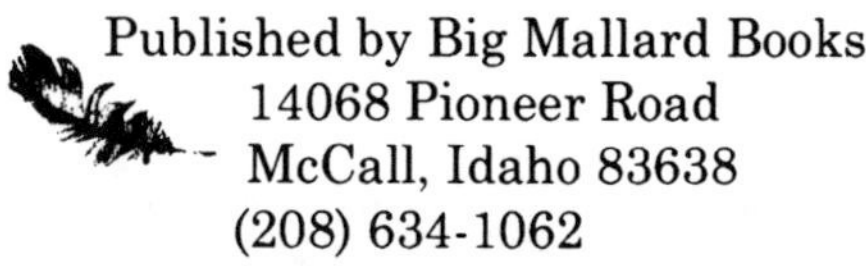
Published by Big Mallard Books
14068 Pioneer Road
McCall, Idaho 83638
(208) 634-1062

Second Printing 2004

Maps by Peter Preston
Photographs by Kathy Deinhardt Hill
Edited by Frances Ford

ISBN 0-9717256-0-8
LCCN 2001127225

Table of Contents

For the Adventurous

Important Information

Caution

Every effort was made to ensure that the information in this book is correct. However, the author and publisher do not assume, and hereby disclaim, any liability to any party for loss or damage caused by errors, omissions, misleading information, or problems caused by the information contained in this guide. Also, participants in the activities suggested by this book must assume the responsibility for their own actions and safety. The information contained in this book cannot take the place of sound judgment and good decision making. The scope of the book does not allow for the disclosure of all the potential hazards and risks involved in such activities.

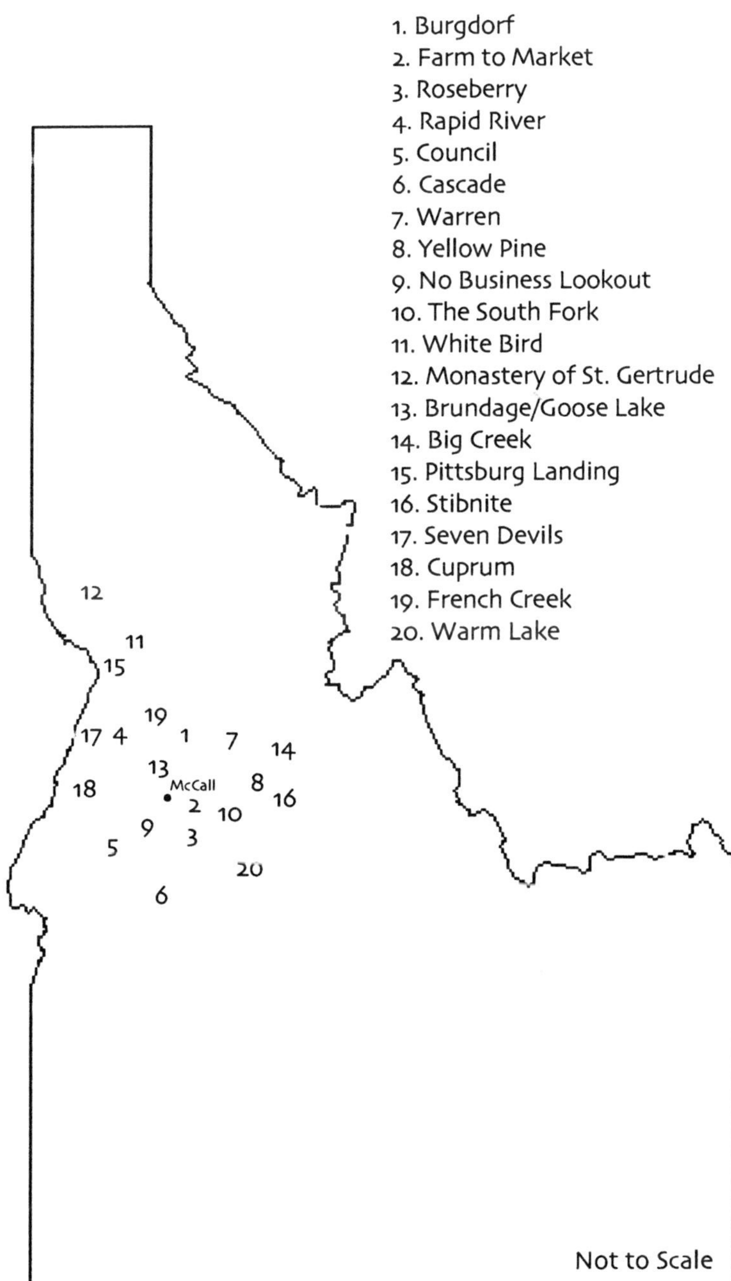

1. Burgdorf
2. Farm to Market
3. Roseberry
4. Rapid River
5. Council
6. Cascade
7. Warren
8. Yellow Pine
9. No Business Lookout
10. The South Fork
11. White Bird
12. Monastery of St. Gertrude
13. Brundage/Goose Lake
14. Big Creek
15. Pittsburg Landing
16. Stibnite
17. Seven Devils
18. Cuprum
19. French Creek
20. Warm Lake
12
11
15
19
17 4
1
7
14
13
McCall
8
18
2
16
10
9
3
5
20
6
Not to Scale

Round Trip Meter in Miles from McCall

Roseberry	26
Brundage Mountain	30
Farm to Market	36
Burgdorf	60
No Business Lookout	61
West Mountain Road	70
Warm Lake	82
Council/Fruitvale	82
Warren	86
Rapid River	88
Yellow Pine	102
South Fork	118
French Creek	118
Seven Devils	126
Big Creek	148
Bear/Cuprum	155
White Bird	160
Stibnite	166
Pittsburg Landing	180
Monastery of St. Gertrude	238

Introduction

McCall, Idaho is a vacation paradise. From pristine mountain lakes, to miles of hiking and biking trails, to championship golf courses, visitors to McCall can be overwhelmed with outdoor activities. A person could spend an entire summer in McCall and never experience it all.

Lying in the heart of the Salmon River Range in Central Idaho, McCall is surrounded by the beauty of those mountains. From the beargrass-covered hillsides of early summer to the dazzling colors of early fall, breathtaking scenery awaits anyone willing to venture out on some of McCall's more interesting backroads. These roads, many of them passable only four months of the year, will give the traveler a taste of Idaho's ruggedness and a sense of her beauty.

In addition to the beauty these roads offer, they also lead to rich Idaho history. The mining areas to the north and east were filled with industrious fortune seekers as early as 1862. Their work is evident throughout McCall's backcountry. The mining boom also brought thousands of Chinese immigrants to the area; their influence can be seen in the hills around Warren. Another ethnic group, the Finns, settled just a few miles south of McCall. Their handiwork and their names still mark the roads and landmarks of the area.

McCall's backroads lead to more than destinations; they lead to adventure and inspire both awe and wonder. Whether watching the salmon clearing the falls on Rapid River, walking the back-country runway at Big Creek to spy a moose, or soaking in the soothing, natural hot water of Burgdorf, you will not be disappointed.

While you are encouraged to participate in McCall's recreational activities—hiking, biking, fishing, boating—you are also encouraged to see all the area has to offer. McCall's backroads will take you to places you will never forget.

Warm Lake

Description

For a picnic or an easy afternoon drive, Warm Lake is the perfect destination. A sparkling gem tucked among Central Idaho mountains, the lake features several campgrounds and swimming spots, two lodges, and beautiful scenery.

Distance/Direction/Road Conditions

Well-suited for any vehicle, the road to Warm Lake is a paved, two-lane road with turnouts. It is located forty-one miles southeast of McCall.

Best Time to Travel

Warm Lake is accessible all year, making it a great destination for both summer and winter travelers. Traffic on Friday and Sunday afternoons can be busy, so if you are looking for a relaxing drive, avoid the weekends.

Facilities

Two lodges, the Warm Lake Lodge and the North Fork Lodge, feature cabins, full-service dining rooms, and convenience stores. As in all back-country facilities, operating hours and availability vary day to day. Be sure to call ahead at either (208) 632-3553 or (208) 632-2000.

Camping

Three Forest Service campgrounds are located on the lake. One, on North Shore Road, was recently renovated and features a boat ramp, potable water, RV hookups, and pit toilets. Immediately west of the North Fork Lodge is a small campground on a hill overlooking the lake. With a beautiful view of the lake, this is a great site for a picnic. Picnic tables, water, and a pit toilet are available.

The third campground is located one-half mile past North Shore Road. Situated away from the lake it features several camping and picnic sites.

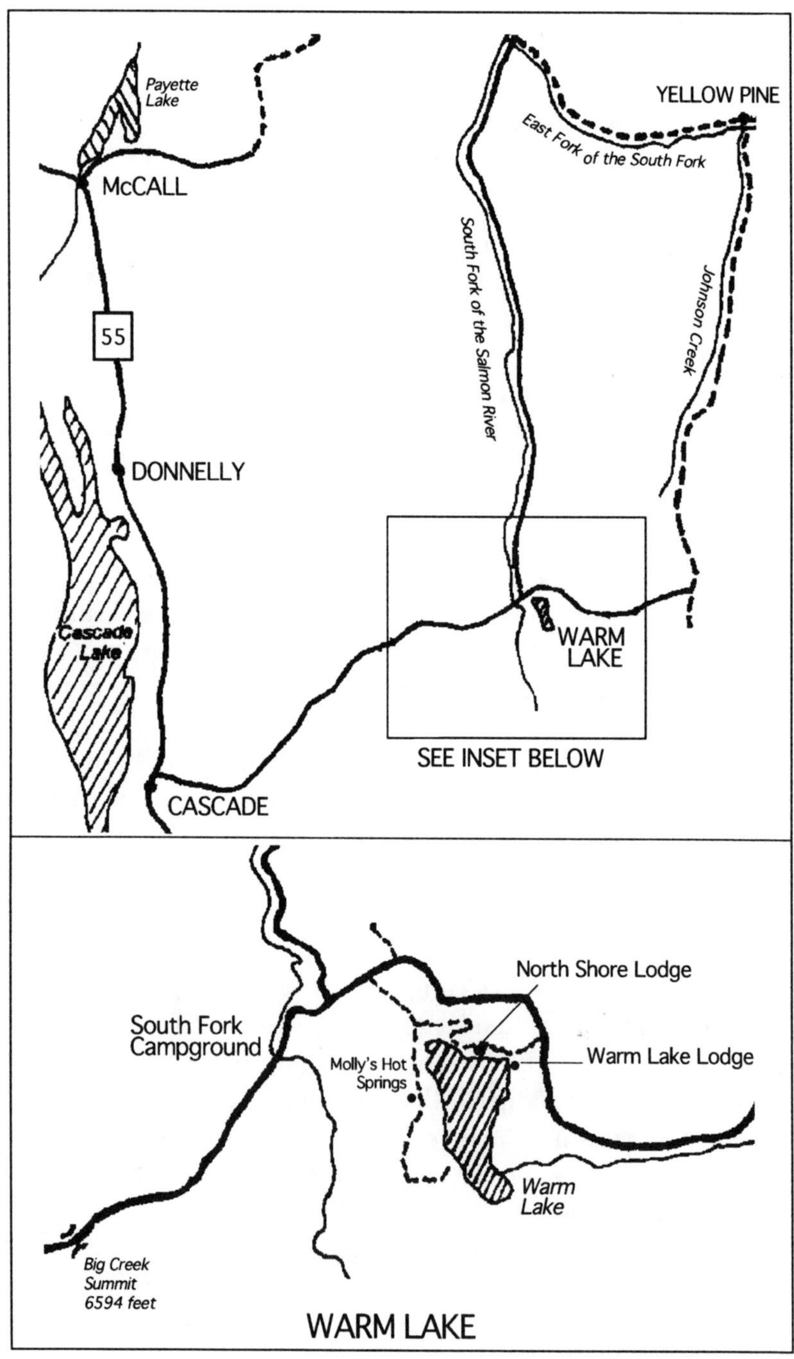
Payette Lake
McCALL
55
DONNELLY
Cascade Lake
CASCADE
YELLOW PINE
East Fork of the South Fork
South Fork of the Salmon River
Johnson Creek
WARM LAKE
SEE INSET BELOW
North Shore Lodge
South Fork Campground
Molly's Hot Springs
Warm Lake Lodge
Warm Lake
Big Creek Summit 6594 feet
WARM LAKE

On the Way

Donnelly, eleven miles into the trip, features a convenience store, a great bakery, and several restaurants

Scott Valley is a beautiful high-mountain valley settled by Sylvester Scott and his wife Malinda. They had 19 children.

Big Creek Summit—elevation 6,594 feet

South Fork Campground lies on the banks of the South Fork of the Salmon River. It is a good place to picnic if you like peace and quiet and the sound of running water.

Molly's Hot Springs is only three miles from Warm Lake on FS Road 474. Take FS Road 474 for 1.5 miles. The hot springs will be on your right. Keep your eye out for eight bathtubs lined up along the creek. Water temperature here has been recorded as high as 114 degrees Fahrenheit.

Billy Kline's Grave—Originally a miner, Kline became a farmer after suffering severe injuries in a blast at the Thunder Mountain mine. He raised potatoes on twenty acres near this site and sold them to the miners in the Thunder Mountain area. Kline died at Knox in 1911.

Knox, located one-quarter mile north on the South Fork Road, was the earliest settlement in the area. The lodge and several cabins are still standing. It is now a heliport for the Forest Service.

Caution

Because of the good condition of the road surface, drivers have a tendency to travel too fast, especially on the tight corners of Big Creek Summit.

Warm Lake is home to deer, elk, and moose. The deer and elk are especially plentiful and can be seen from early spring to late fall, often crossing the highway to reach the marshy grasses surrounding the lake.

Getting There

From McCall, head eleven miles south on Highway 55, through Donnelly and on to the north end of Cascade. Prior to entering Cascade, the Warm Lake Road will take off to the left (east). Take this road and follow it twenty-six miles to Warm

The old hotel at Knox

Lake. Road signs will direct you to the various lodges and campgrounds in the Warm Lake area.

Miscellaneous

The Forest Service maintains control over land in the Warm Lake area; however, federal leases allow for many private homes around the lake. Take this into consideration before wandering into someone's living space.

Warm Lake is home to a large moose population, and many visitors get the opportunity to see these magnificent animals.

But moose can be unpredictable. If you see one, do not approach it on foot. While no fatalities have been recorded at Warm Lake, moose can kill people.

History

While Warm Lake is a picturesque spot tucked between Idaho mountains, its settlement was one of convenience for miners and freighters heading to the lucrative mining areas of Thunder Mountain.

John Wesley Knox may have been the first white man in the Warm Lake area, prospecting there as early as 1890 when he staked twelve claims in what is now known as the Knox townsite, approximately three miles north of Warm Lake. At that time, maps of the area indicated a "Hot Lake" located near the South Fork of the Salmon River. Speculation abounds as to the origin of the name "Warm Lake," but the numerous hot springs in the area certainly justify the name. The high concentration of hot springs is attributed to a fault line that follows the South Fork. However, do not be deceived. Warm Lake is as cold as the high mountain streams that feed it.

Knox apparently left the area in the late 1890s, giving way to Charles Randall. Randall filed mining claims, built the first structures, and attempted to rename the area "Randall," but the name did not stick. Randall established a hotel, store, and stable, and hosted miners heading to the Big Creek and Thunder Mountain mining areas, as well as the Thunderbolt Mine just north of Knox. The Knox post office operated from 1904 to 1908 and serviced 200 residents.

Randall left the area in 1910, selling his properties to Bill and Molly Kessler who arrived in 1907 from Long Valley. The two continued to operate the hotel until 1912 when Daniel Robinette (Robnette) arrived and claimed he owned the property. A court battle ensued, and the Kesslers lost. Undeterred, the Kesslers built a road from Knox to the shores of Warm Lake. They settled at the site of the present Warm Lake Lodge and in 1911 began construction on the first hotel on the lake. To supplement their income until the hotel became a viable business, Molly Kessler established a fox farm, earning as much as $175 for a good pelt. Once the hotel became a popular resort, Molly closed the fox farm and became a full-time host. The Kesslers owned the hotel until 1939.

At Knox, Robinette filed for a homestead patent on the land, but abandoned the place in 1916. Daniel Drake took over the site, also filed for a homestead, and received a patent in 1922. He continued to run the lodge and worked the area as a packer until 1929, when he sold out to Benjamin Seward. Seward took over the lodge, only to have it burn to the ground in the early 1930s. He rebuilt and that building remains standing at the edge of the clearing at the old Knox townsite.

Cabins around Warm Lake began appearing in 1925, first on the east side of the lake. By 1933, cabins were going up regularly on the west side of the lake. The automobile, along with better roads into the area, made Knox and Warm Lake more than just stopovers for people heading into the mining areas of Stibnite. They became destinations for people seeking a mountain getaway.

The Civilian Conservation Corps added to the area's population in 1933 when a CCC camp was established at the site now known as Project Camp. The Corps constructed the first water system at Warm Lake, some of which is still used today. They also built a swimming pool on the banks of the South Fork of the Salmon River, just north of Warm Lake. The pool, called the Warm Lake Plunge, was heated with water from Duke Hot Springs and featured showers, changing rooms, and bath houses. The pool was open to the public until 1973 when the state health department closed it. It has since been filled in; only the top of the pool walls is still visible.

The 1930s saw other developments at Warm Lake, including the construction of Campbell's Camp, now known as the North Shore Lodge. Articles in the Cascade newspaper promoted Warm Lake as "one of the most beautiful spots in Idaho" and an "ideal place for rest and recreation."

Eventually cabins were built in the Paradise Valley area,

adjacent to the Knox townsite. Roads were improved, electricity was provided, phone service became available. Over the years, the area became a place of vacation homes and guest residences, as evident in the 1960 census. Knox recorded a population of ten, followed by Warm Lake with eight.

Today, many of the old cabins built in the '30s remain, weekend getaways for second and third generations of the earliest Warm Lake residents. The North Shore and Warm Lake Lodges still open their doors to guests providing a rustic, central Idaho experience. Even the old lodge at Knox and several of the original cabins remain, visible reminders of Warm Lake's rugged, yet significant past.

For More Information

Warm Lake Lodge
Warm Lake, Idaho 83611
(208) 632-3553

North Shore Lodge and Resort
175 Shoreline
Warm Lake, Idaho 83611
(208) 632-2000

Cascade Ranger District
Boise National Forest
P.O. Box 696
Cascade, Idaho
(208) 382-4271

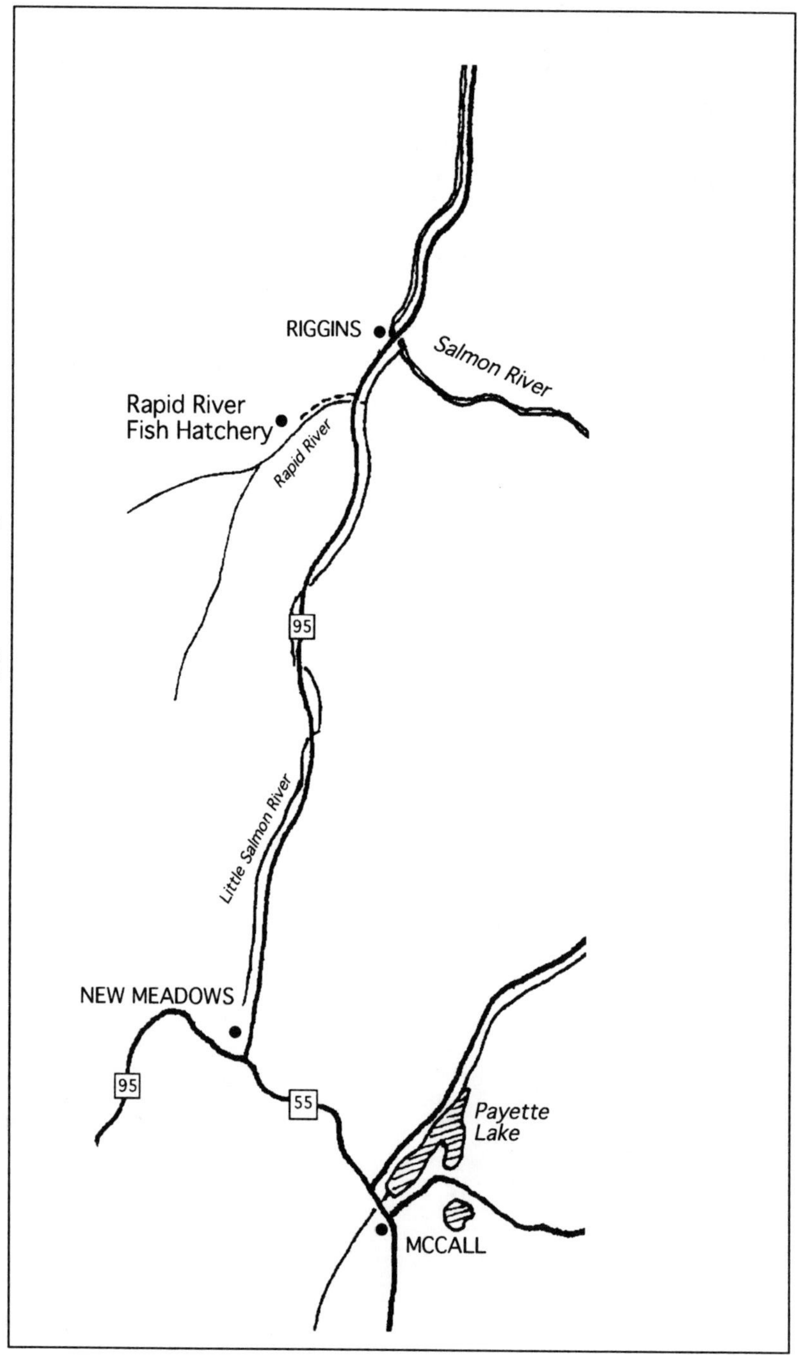
RIGGINS
Salmon River
Rapid River
Fish Hatchery
Rapid River
95
Little Salmon River
NEW MEADOWS
95
55
Payette
Lake
MCCALL

Rapid River Fish Hatchery

Description

The Rapid River Fish Hatchery is the largest spring Chinook salmon hatchery in Idaho. Located northwest of McCall near the town of Riggins, the hatchery provides a look at man's efforts to save these amazing fish.

Distance/Direction/Conditions

Located forty-four miles northwest of McCall off Highway 95, this trip is on paved roads all the way, making it suitable for any vehicle.

Best Time to Travel

The fish are running up Rapid River from early May until early September. May and June are typically the times of the biggest runs and offer the mildest temperatures for a visit to the hatchery. The fish are spawned at the hatchery in September, another good time to visit.

Facilities

A well-maintained picnic area is available at the hatchery along with public restrooms and drinking water.

Camping

None is available.

On the Way

One rest area is located on Highway 95 at Mile 38.

Pottenger's Market is located at the corner of Highway 95 and Rapid River Road. It is a great place to pick up snacks or drinks before heading to the hatchery.

Riggins lies four miles north of the hatchery on Highway 95. There you will find restaurants, grocery stores, and gas stations.

Caution

Highways 55 and 95 are narrow in spots and can be crowded

with vacation traffic. Don't get in a hurry.

Getting there

From the northwest edge of McCall, follow Highway 55 to New Meadows. In New Meadows, turn right (north) on to Highway 95. After a few miles, you will begin following the Little Salmon River as it winds its way to the Main Salmon. Approximately forty-one miles into the trip, you will come to the intersection of Highway 95 and Rapid River Road, also known as Fish Hatchery Road. Pottenger's Market will be on your left. Turn left (west) on to Rapid River Road. Follow this road for approximately 2.5 miles. It will take you to the fish hatchery. All roads to the hatchery are well marked.

Miscellaneous Information

In addition to the hatchery, you can also visit the fish trap, located one-half mile west of Highway 95 on Rapid River Road. Here you can see a truly inspiring sight: salmon trying to hurdle the man-made falls in Rapid River. The falls is located directly behind (south) of the fish trap. A short trail takes you from the trap's parking area to the falls. Ask the employees at the fish hatchery about this trail. It is worth the effort.

History

The struggles of the Idaho salmon have been well-documented ever since the first dam, Bonneville, was built on the Columbia River in 1938. But three dams on the Snake River—Hell's Canyon, Oxbow, and Brownlee—led to the creation of the Rapid River Fish Hatchery. Operated by the Idaho Department of Fish and Game, with funding from Idaho Power Company, the hatchery attempts to mitigate the lost Chinook runs on the Salmon, Payette, Boise, and Weiser Rivers and their tributaries.

The hatchery was constructed in 1964, following the completion of Oxbow and Brownlee dams. Hell's Canyon dam was completed in 1968. None of the dams have facilities that allow for the passage of fish; thus the Federal Energy Regulatory Commission requires Idaho Power to compensate for the loss of the fish runs. To do so, each year the company is required to produce and release three million salmon smolts at the hatchery.

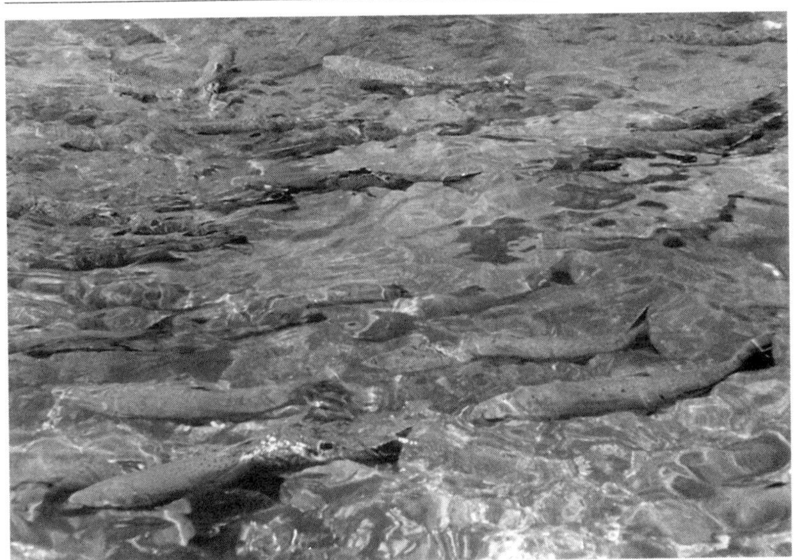

Chinook salmon at Rapid River Hatchery pool

In addition, some of the smolts (between 100,000 and one million) are released below Hells Canyon Dam to aid salmon runs in Oregon streams.

Salmon that return to Rapid River between May and mid-July are considered spring Chinook. These fish are trapped by Fish and Game workers, then transferred to holding ponds at the hatchery. Here they are cared for until mid-August. Then the eggs are harvested and fertilized. Fish that arrive at the trap after mid-July are considered summer Chinook. They are captured at the fish trap but then released back into Rapid River to preserve a native salmon run.

To meet production goals, between 2,500 to 3,000 adult salmon must return to Rapid River. The best return was in 2001, when over 22,000 salmon survived the 600 mile trip from the ocean.

Once the eggs are harvested and fertilized, they are placed in incubators where they are exposed to the water from Rapid River. They remain in the incubators until they hatch. When the small fish, "fry," are able to swim and search for food, they are transferred to the outdoor raceways where they are fed. They remain here until they are approximately two inches long. At this point the fish are moved into the larger rearing ponds, capable of holding more than 500,000 fish. The fish are held in these ponds until they are ready to be released and begin their migration to the Pacific. The entire process—from fertilization to release—takes about eighteen months.

Since fish-raising is a year-round production, the hatchery is open daily, 7 a.m. to 4 p.m., with Fish and Game personnel available to answer questions. Informal tours are available on request when you arrive at the hatchery and take about thirty minutes. If you have a big group, however, call ahead and schedule a formal tour. The tour is free, as is use of the picnic area.

For More Information

Rapid River Fish Hatchery
Riggins, Idaho 83549
(208) 628-3277

West Mountain Road to Cascade

Description

The county seat of Valley County, Cascade sits on the shores of Cascade Lake, a reservoir created in the 1940s. Although originally a lumber town, with the closure of the Boise Cascade mill in the spring of 2001, the town now depends on tourism and county business for its livelihood. It is a favorite spot for snowmobilers in winter, featuring over 800 miles of groomed trails.

Distance/Direction/Road Conditions

The back road to Cascade runs south along the west side of Long Valley. Round trip from McCall is seventy miles with a mix of paved and improved gravel roads.

Best Time to Travel

In the summer, Cascade Lake's shores are filled with outdoor enthusiasts, especially on the weekends. For spectacular scenery and breathtaking colors, fall is best as the aspen trees put on quite a show.

Facilities

Cascade offers all services, including some excellent restaurants scattered along Main Street. A delightful nine-hole golf course sits on the shores of Cascade Lake.

Camping

Camping and picnic spots abound on the shores of Cascade Lake. Operated by Idaho State Parks and Recreation, visitors can find over 300 camping and picnic spots around the lake. All campgrounds feature restroom facilities and potable water. Some have RV hookups.

On the Way

Tamarack Resort, at Mile 19, offers hiking, biking, and cross

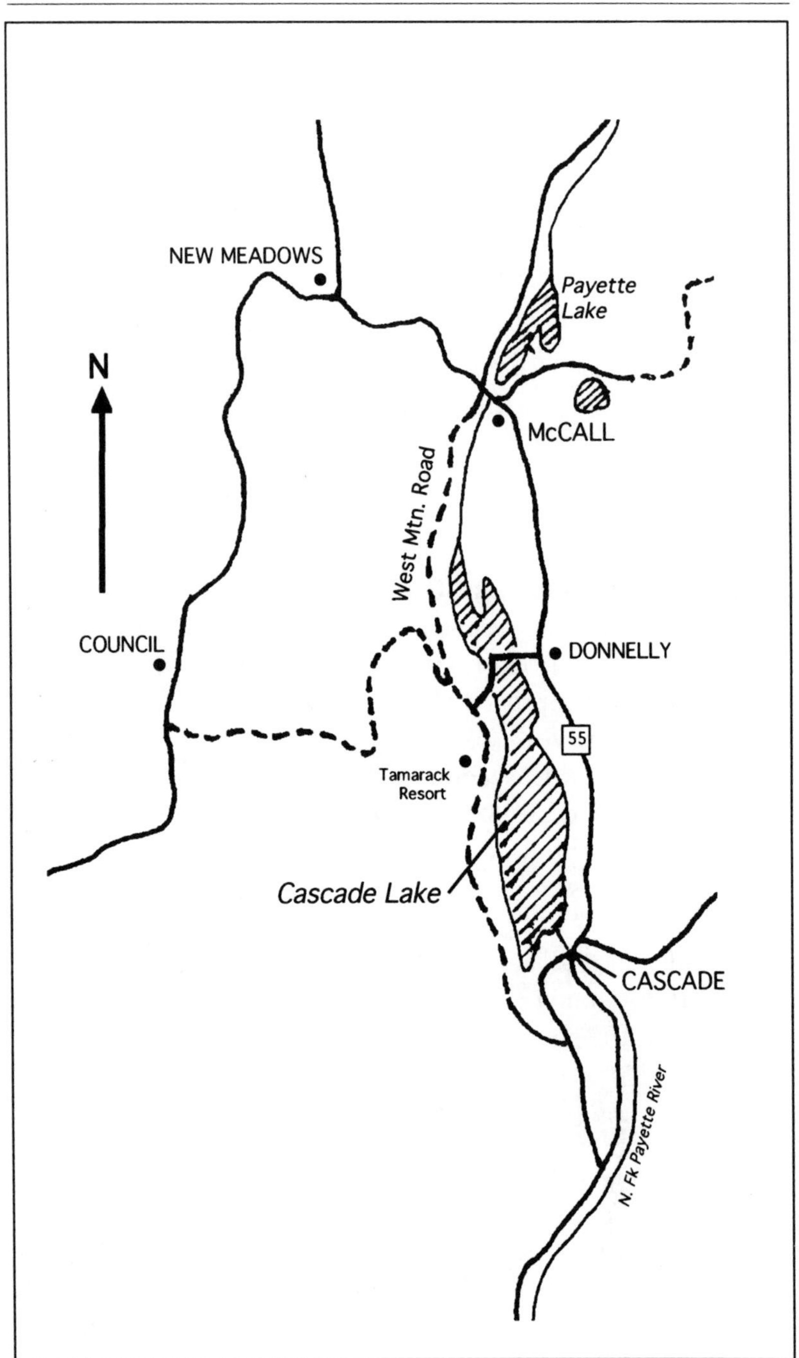
NEW MEADOWS
Payette Lake
N
McCALL
West Mtn. Road
COUNCIL
DONNELLY
55
Tamarack Resort
Cascade Lake
CASCADE
N. Fk Payette River

country ski trails. A small restaurant is also located at the resort site. Call (208) 325-1000 for information.

Cascade Golf Course, Mile 40, can challenge any golfer. Tee times can be arranged by calling (208) 382-4835.

Caution

West Mountain Road runs through open range and local ranchers and herders use the road frequently to move stock. Cars must yield to the animals.

Numerous summer homes are located on the southwest end of Cascade Lake and in the summer, traffic can be heavy, especially on weekends.

Getting There

From the northwest end of McCall, on Highway 55, turn left onto Boydstun Street. After 1.5 miles, turn right onto West Valley Road; this will veer left and become Wisdom Road. At two miles, turn right on to West Mountain Road, a well-maintained county road.

West Mountain Road will wander along the west edge of Long Valley and follow the North Fork of the Payette River. At Mile 17, the road turns to pavement. Continue to head south, passing several well-maintained state parks and campgrounds. At Mile 20, the road once again turns to gravel. Here the views of Cascade Lake become more expansive. At Mile 34, the road turns to pavement and heads into the Cascade summer home area. At the south end of the lake, the road will turn east. At Mile 37.5, turn left onto Lakeshore Drive and head north toward Cascade. You will pass several campgrounds and picnic areas. The Cascade golf course is located at Mile 40. Immediately after the golf course club house, turn right and follow this street to Highway 55. At the highway, turn left and return the thirty miles to McCall.

Miscellaneous Information

Cascade Lake is known for its fine fishing, almost anytime of year. Rainbow trout, perch, and small mouth bass are ready for the taking. In the summer, many fishermen bring out their boats to cover the lake, but fish can also be caught from the land. In the winter, the lake freezes over and on sunny days, the ice is dotted with hardy fishermen looking to catch their limits. Another great fishing spot is just below the Cascade Dam spillway. Fishermen often crowd the bridge here to try their luck. Contact Tackle Tom's at (208) 382-4367 for the latest fishing report.

History

Cascade owes its existence to the Idaho Northern Branch of the Short Line Railroad, which pushed its way into Central Idaho's high mountain valleys in 1913. As the railroad inched toward McCall, its final destination, it followed a route that missed several well-established communities. Two new towns resulted, Cascade and Donnelly.

Cascade was created from Thunder City, Van Wyck, and Crawford. Thunder City was located at the present intersection of Highway 55 and Gold Dust Road, six miles south of Cascade. It served as a way station and outfitting spot for miners heading to Thunder Mountain. Van Wyck, the first settlement in Long Valley, was situated one mile west of present Cascade. Remnants of Crawford are still visible today, just northeast of Cascade on the Warm Lake Road.

Cascade was platted in 1913, a total of six blocks. Then the migration began. Rather than build new structures, area merchants relocated their businesses, buildings and all, to the new town. The post office was moved from Crawford; Thunder City gave up the Methodist Church, Cromwell's Blacksmith Shop and Logue's General Store. Van Wyck donated the drug store and the Baptist church which later became the first Cascade school. The bigger buildings were taken apart, the pieces marked, and then reassembled in Cascade. The small buildings were moved to their new sites on skids.

While Cascade flourished, Van Wyck, Crawford, and Thunder City faded. Van Wyck held on the longest, maintaining a grade school into the 1940s.

With the railroad and an ample timber supply, Cascade caught the attention of lumber men. The Boise Payette Lumber

Company arrived in 1916 and soon established logging camps around Cascade including Cabarton, MacGregor, Scott Valley, and Clear Creek. Harry Morrison and his crews constructed spur lines to the camps. Originally logs were sent by rail to mills in Emmett. In 1924, Cascade's mill was built. It changed hands several times before Boise Cascade took it over.

Cascade flourished. In 1915, the first school was opened. The town's first newspaper, *The Cascade News,* started publication in 1916. Valley County was formed in 1917, and Cascade was named the county seat. Farming and the timber industry provided the backbone of the economy.

Cascade Reservoir came into existence in the 1940s with the construction of Cascade Dam, an earth-filled structure ninety feet high and 785 feet long. The dam, operated by the Bureau of Reclamation, is part of the Black Canyon Irrigation Project. The dam holds a water storage area of 700,000 acre feet and supplies water to more than 25,000 acres of farmland.

Construction on the dam began in the fall of 1941, but World War II interrupted the project when materials became unavailable. Work resumed following the war, and the dam was completed in July 1948. An Idaho Power facility has been generating power from the site since January 1949.

The dam was the final blow to Van Wyck. While it survived the railroad, it could not survive the backwater created by the dam. Today the townsite of Van Wyck lies under the waters of the reservoir, now officially called Cascade Lake.

The Boise Cascade mill closure of 2001 was a major blow to Cascade's economy, but the townspeople remain upbeat. The pleasant summers and snow-filled winters make Cascade a vacationer's playground and well worth a visit.

For More Information

Cascade Lake State Park
P.O. Box 709
Cascade, Idaho 83611
(208) 382-6544

Cascade Golf Course
(208) 382-4835

Cascade Chamber of Commerce
(208) 382-3833

Farm to Market

Description

At one time, this route was the main thoroughfare for homesteaders and farmers living in Long Valley. Remains of old Finnish homesteads can still be seen, along with some panoramic rural scenery.

Distance/Direction/Conditions

Farm to Market Road is a thirty-five mile drive encompassing the east side of Long Valley, south of McCall. All but six miles of the road are paved.

Best time to Travel

The scenery on this route changes continually, although mornings and evenings are the most scenic. A fall trip offers the beauty of the valley's aspen groves and mountains' tamarack forests.

Facilities

Restrooms are available in Roseberry.

Donnelly features several good restaurants, a bakery, and a convenience store.

Camping

None

On the way

The Elo School house, at Mile 1.5, was the first Finnish school in Long Valley.

Finnish Church and cemetery

Black Pine Deer Farm

Bell Cemetery, former site of Spink, an early Finnish Community

Roseberry, see page 95.

Caution

Watch out for deer and elk, any time on this road. Also, this is open range country, so farm animals have the right-of-way.

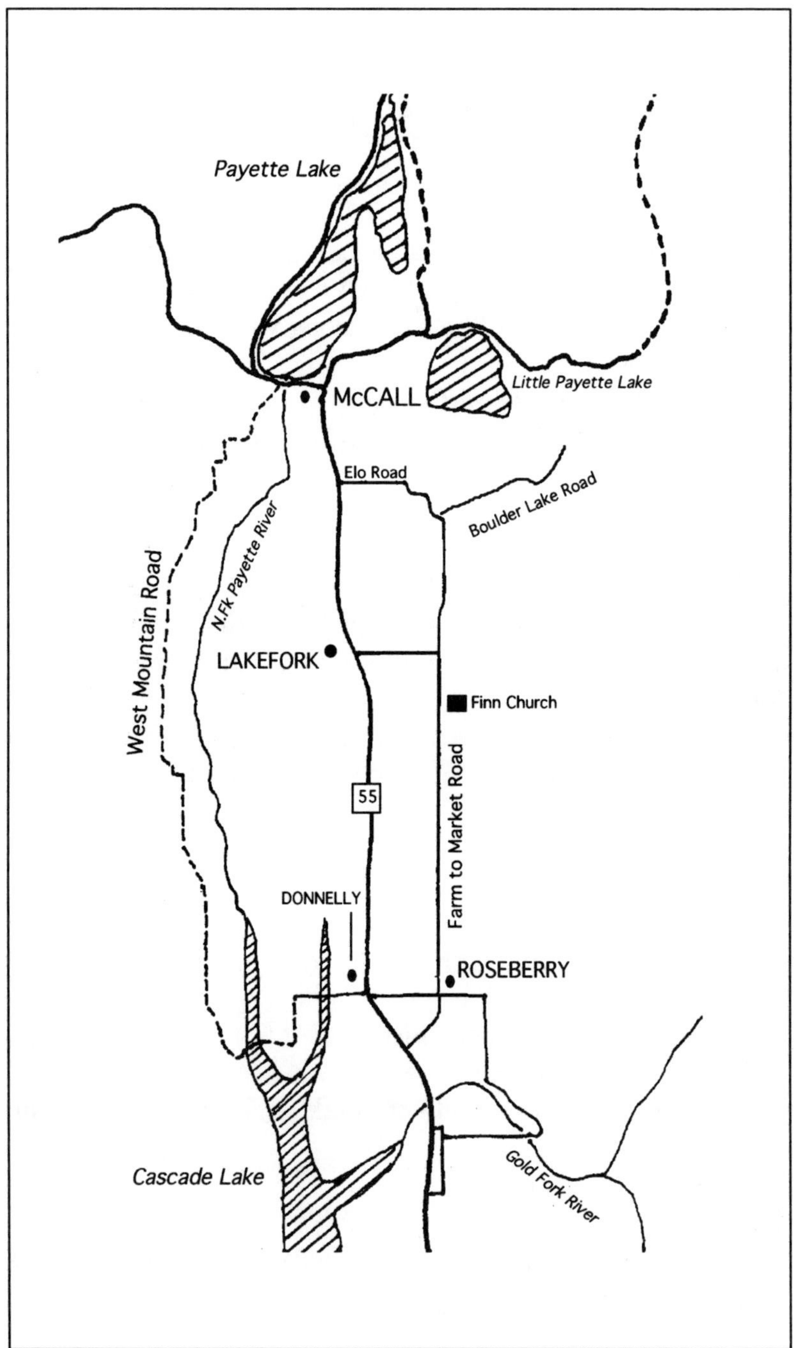
Payette Lake
McCALL
Little Payette Lake
Elo Road
Boulder Lake Road
N.Fk Payette River
West Mountain Road
LAKEFORK
Finn Church
55
Farm to Market Road
DONNELLY
ROSEBERRY
Cascade Lake
Gold Fork River

Getting there

From the south end of McCall, head south on Highway 55 for one mile. Turn left (east) on Elo Road. At the third mile, Elo Road will fork. Stay to the right, and you are now on Farm to Market Road. Follow it until you reach Roseberry, at Mile 13.6. Here turn left (east) on to East Roseberry Road. Follow East Roseberry road for one mile. It will make a sharp turn right (south) and become Gold Fork Road. Stay on Gold Fork Road for five miles as it follows the Gold Fork River. At Mile 18.2, turn right on Davis Creek Road at the bridge that crosses Gold Fork. Follow this road until it comes to a T. Either direction will take you back to Highway 55. On Highway 55, head north, back to McCall.

Miscellaneous

Visitors are welcome to wander the Finnish and Spink Cemeteries. The Black Pine Deer Farm, a commercial fallow deer operation, is open to the public for guided tours. Visitors must call ahead for reservations.

History

While the Finnish people were not the first settlers in McCall and Long Valley, they certainly had a strong influence in the development of the area. Most of the land between McCall and Cascade was originally homesteaded by these enterprising people who farmed and carved a niche for themselves in Idaho's mountain valleys.

The Finns arrived in 1896, when three families—the Lahtis, Haralas, and Koskelas—came to Long Valley from Oregon. They were soon followed by other Finnish families who came from the mining areas of Minnesota and Wyoming. However, some of those who traveled to Long Valley came directly from Finland. They were attracted to the area because land was still available for homesteading, and timber was readily accessible in the nearby mountains. Long Valley also is said to have resembled their homeland.

After 1900, the majority of Finns settled on the east side of Long Valley. Between 1904 and 1925, ninety homestead pat-

Finn Church

ents were granted to Finnish settlers, most of them located along Farm to Market Road. In 1915, eighty-five Finnish families called Long Valley home. On first arrival, the Finns raised cattle, but soon found they could raise wheat, timothy, and clover. They also found the soil of Long Valley compatible with potatoes, and this soon became a cash crop. Still, the long winters made for tough times. In order to survive financially, many Finnish men traveled to Wyoming in the winter months to work in the mines. They would return in the spring to farm. Eventually, they established themselves well enough to remain in the valley the entire year.

Several small Finnish communities were established in the valley, although little remains of them now. Elo, just 1.5 miles from McCall, was founded by Reverend John William Eloheimo, who arrived in the Valley at the turn of the century. A Lutheran minister, he helped found the Finnish Synod of the Lutheran Church of America and held national offices in the organization. He founded Elo in 1905. He opened a store and served as postmaster, justice of the peace, and magistrate. His store doubled as a courtroom.

All that remains of Elo is the old schoolhouse and the teacher's residence. The school, opened in 1906, served the Finnish children in the area, and English was an integral part of their curriculum. Students caught speaking Finn were forced to clean erasers. As Finns moved into the valley, school enrollment increased; by 1916 fifty-four students attended school at Elo. The school operated until the 1950s when students began attending schools in McCall and Donnelly.

One of the most photographed landmarks in Valley County is the Finn Church. Placed on the National Register of Historic Places in 1980, the Finn Church is maintained by the Finnish Ladies' Aid Society. The society, founded in 1904, was the impetus behind the church. After Uriel Kantola donated part of his homestead specifically for a church, the society began collecting money, and by 1916, the group had raised $1811.37, enough to begin construction. The structure was built by volunteers under the direction of John Ruuska and John Heikkila. Buried in the cornerstone of the church are treasures from Finnish families: passports, coins, and pictures. Today the church looks much the same as it did when it was dedicated in the fall of 1917. While regular Sunday services are no longer held there, the church is still used for weddings and funerals.

Saunas, an important part of Finnish culture, are scattered across Long Valley on the old homesteads. Every home had a separate sauna building complete with a barrel or box stove, benches, and water storage. Taking a sauna was not only a way to get clean, but also a form of socializing for the Finns. While many of the saunas have been neglected, a few locals still maintain and use them.

The Finnish influence in Long Valley has declined over the years. The last survivor of the original settlers died in 1979, and the remaining second generation Finns are in their eighties. Still the Ladies' Aid Society attempts to preserve the Finnish culture. They continue to maintain the church, and each June they host a celebration of the summer solstice, St. John's Day, a national holiday in Finland.

For More Information

Black Pine Deer Farm
Farm to Market Road
Donnelly, Idaho 83615
(208) 325-8504

Valley County Museum
13131 Farm To Market Road
Donnelly, Idaho 83615
(208) 325-8628

Brundage Mountain and Goose Lake Road

Description

Brundage Mountain and Goose Lake are well known as part of McCall's winter paradise. However, upgrades to the road, the mountain facilities, and camping sites at the lake make this route a nice afternoon trip in the summer and early fall. Do not pass up the opportunity to ride the chairlift to the top of Brundage, where remarkable views of Payette Lake, Meadows Valley, and the Seven Devils await you.

Distance/Direction/Road Conditions

Located north of McCall, the road is paved for eight miles, to the entrance of the Brundage Mountain ski area. From there, an improved dirt road leads seven more miles to Goose Lake.

Facilities

During the summer, Brundage Mountain Corporation opens its lifts to mountain bikers and sight-seers. Tickets for a trip up the mountain are $8 for adults. Seniors get a discount at $5 per trip.

Brundage also offers guests snacks, cold drinks, and restroom facilities. The hill is open Fridays 1-6 p.m. and weekends, 11 a.m. to 6 p.m.

The Forest Service operates a campground at Goose Lake. Fire rings, picnic tables, and pit toilets are available.

Best Time to Travel

Goose Lake is best to visit on weekdays, when you may have the entire lake to yourself. The chairlift at Brundage is open to sight-seers Friday through Saturday, beginning July 4 and running through Labor Day.

Camping

The Forest Service was renovating a campground on the south

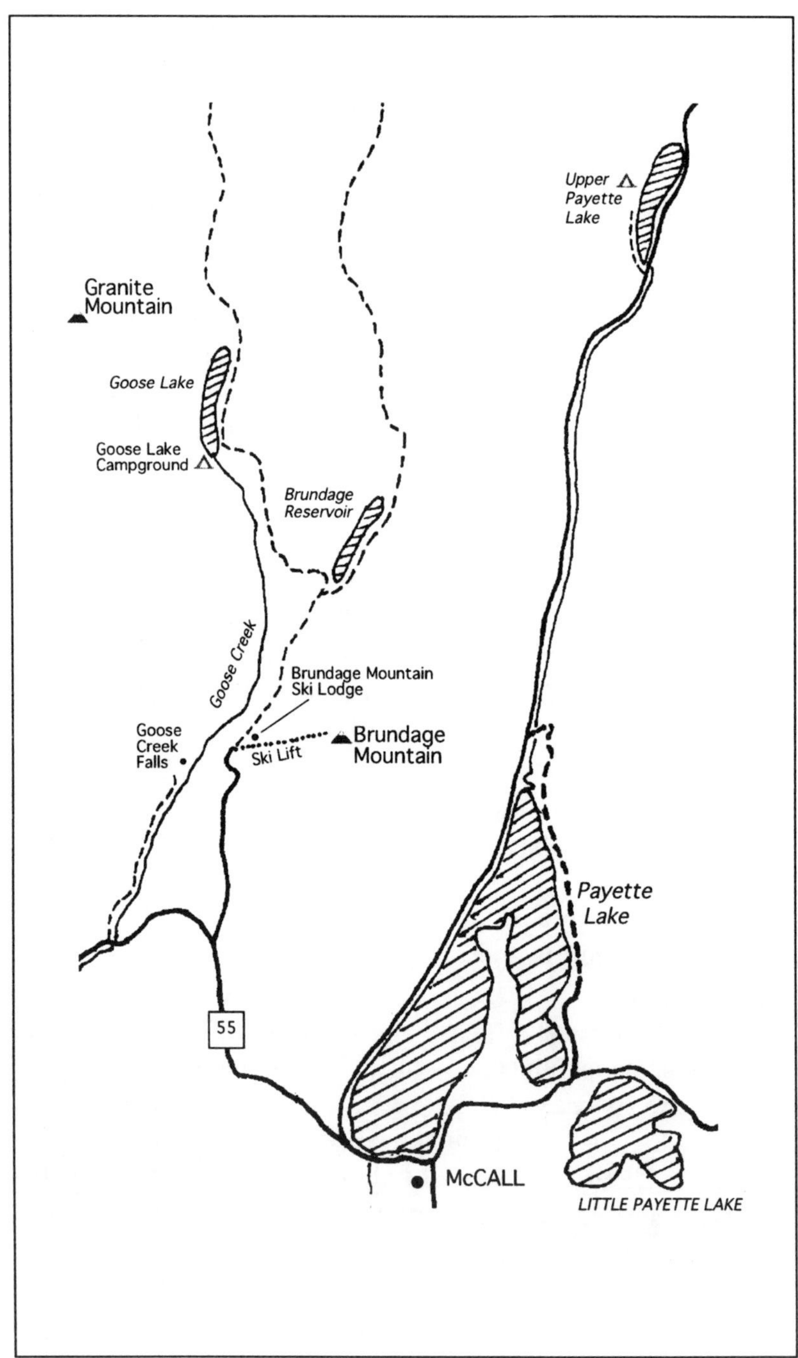
Upper
Payette
Lake
Granite
Mountain
Goose Lake
Goose Lake
Campground
Brundage
Reservoir
Goose Creek
Brundage Mountain
Ski Lodge
Goose
Creek
Falls
Ski Lift
Brundage
Mountain
Payette
Lake
55
McCALL
LITTLE PAYETTE LAKE

end of Goose Lake during the summer of 2001. An additional camping and picnic area is also located on the lake, just off the road. For those who want to explore, Hazard Lake, twelve miles further, offers campsites and picnic tables.

On the Way

McCall's Little Ski Hill, located two miles north of McCall on Highway 55, is home to McCall's Mitey Mites, a local organization which promotes competitive skiing for the youth of McCall. Many of McCall's skiers, Olympians included, honed their skills on the Little Hill. Presently operated by the Payette Lakes Ski Club, the Hill is a non-profit venture established in 1937.

Bear Creek Lodge offers rooms in a picturesques setting for McCall area visitors.

Goose Creek Falls trailhead leads to a short but steep hike to a beautiful waterfall.

Brundage Dam and Reservoir, part of an extensive irrigation system, is open to visitors who can drive right to the dam. Pit toilets are available at this site.

Caution

While Brundage Mountain Road is in excellent condition, it contains some hairpin curves. Pay attention to the speed signs for each corner; they are accurate. Also, be aware that when the pavement is wet, it can be slick.

The dirt section of the road, especially the two miles immediately following the ski area, can be a washboard. Also be aware of falling rock through this area.

Getting There

From the northwest end of McCall, head north on Highway 55. After 4.4 miles, you will see the well-marked, paved road to Brundage on your right. Take this road and follow it six miles to the Brundage Mountain Resort entrance. Here the road forks. You can go straight ahead to the Brundage Mountain parking lot or take the left fork, which will lead to Goose Lake, 3.5 miles further.

Miscellaneous Information

Brundage Mountain is best known for its incredible powder

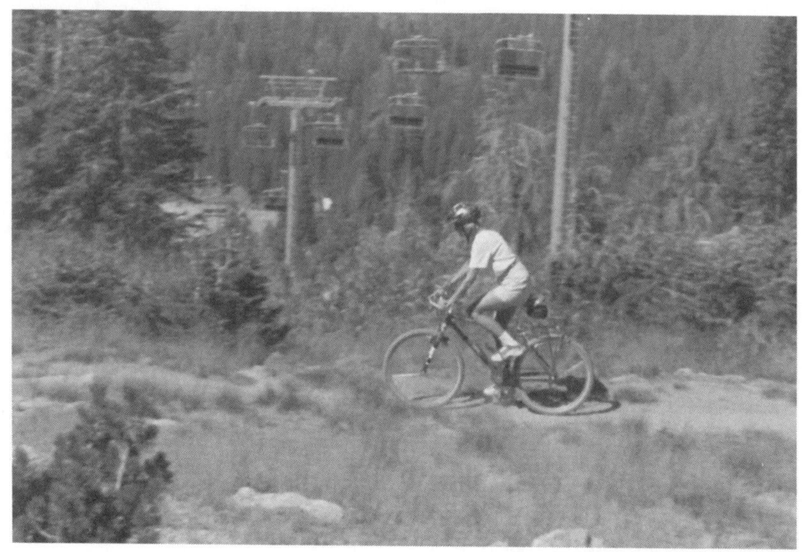

Brundage offers great views and great rides.

skiing in the winter. In recent years, Brundage has earned a reputation as a mountain biker's dream, with trails for both novice and expert bikers. Beyond the physical activities served by the mountain, Brundage has become the newest concert site in McCall, hosting a variety of musical performances. Food and drinks are catered at these events which take place throughout the summer. Call Brundage Mountain or the McCall Chamber of Commerce at (208) 634-7631 for concert dates.

History

While Brundage clearly is McCall's winter showpiece, it was not the first ski hill in McCall. That distinction goes to the Little Ski Hill, two miles north of McCall.

The Little Hill, as it is fondly known, was the brain child of Warren Brown, long-time McCall entrepreneur. After Sun Valley established its ski hill in 1936, Brown decided that McCall, with its abundant snowfall, could also benefit from a ski hill. Originally, the little hill focused on Nordic events—cross-country skiing and ski-jumping—under the direction of Corey Engen. But with the urging of Brown, Engen introduced downhill skiing to McCall and soon the Little Hill became home to skiers of all persuasions.

The Little Hill was the perfect spot for novice skiers, but eventually, experienced skiers found it less than challenging. When J. R. Simplot, a frequent skier at the Little Hill, dropped the hint that a bigger hill was needed, both Engen and Brown listened. Simplot, a well-known Idaho industrialist, offered his financial support for the new venture. In the late 1950s, Engen went in search of the perfect hill and found it on Brundage Mountain.

The Payette National Forest controlled Brundage Mountain. The mountain had been previously logged, which was a benefit, as the early logging roads gave access to the hill. Engen hiked up the mountain several times, trying to get a feel for the terrain. In his mind he laid out the runs, pictured a site for the lodge, and planned the first chairlift. With plan in hand, he headed to the Forest Service for its approval. The Forest Service agreed, and in early 1961 issued a permit to Engen, Simplot, and Brown to operate a ski resort on Brundage Mountain.

Work began in earnest. Men from the Brown Tie and Lumber Company were sent to the hill to clear two runs, build a parking lot, and level an area for the lodge. A Forest Service engineer was brought in to survey a straight line for the chair lift. While work crews cleared the area, Engen headed to Spokane where he purchased the hill's first lift from the Riblet Lift Company.

The lift and the lodge, an A-frame structure built by Frank Brown, Warren's son, were completed in the fall of 1961. When the hill opened for business in November of the same year, Idaho Governor Robert Smylie took part in the festivities. Skiers found two runs, North and South (now called Main Street and Alpine), a two-seat lift, and a cozy lodge. Even better, a lift ticket for an entire day of skiing cost $3.50.

Over the years, Brundage Mountain Corporation has made constant improvements to the hill to accommodate skiers. A second chair was added in the 1970s and the lodge was remodeled in 1983. Additional runs were also built. In 1990, the Centennial triple chairlift was added and in 1997, the high-speed quad made it possible for skiers to reach the top of the mountain in just eight minutes. With the mountain's 7,640 foot elevation, skiers enjoy a vertical drop of 1,800 feet and 1,300 acres of ski trails.

Brundage Mountain Corporation has also expanded recreational opportunities on the hill. In 1989, snowcat skiing was introduced, opening the backside of the mountain to those who love to ski powder. In the summer of 1995 mountain bikers were given the chance to challenge the mountain with a variety of trails from expert to novice. The bicycle community responded and now the hill hosts NORBA sponsored downhill and cross-country races.

McCall's mountain location and its long winters make it the perfect location for a ski resort. With the foresight of Brundage Mountain's managers, the hill now provides recreation and sightseeing opportunities for summer tourists as well.

For Further Information

Brundage Mountain Resort
P. O. Box 1062
1410 Mill Road
McCall, Idaho 83638
Business Office (208) 634-4151
Brundage Mountain (208) 634-7462
Snow Report (208) 634-7669
1-800-888-7544

Payette National Forest
McCall Ranger District
P.O. Box 1062
102 W. Lake Street
McCall, Idaho 83638
(208) 634-0400

Yellow Pine

Description

Yellow Pine is a back-country community with approximately forty full time residents. Settled in the early 1900s as a supply center and stopover for miners and ranchers in Idaho's wilderness, it features a cordial atmosphere and beautiful scenery.

Distance/Direction/Road Conditions

The community of Yellow Pine is located fifty-one miles east of McCall on Lick Creek/FS Road 48. Recent improvements to the road have resulted in seven miles of pavement, then improved dirt road the remainder of the route.

The road is narrow in some places and extremely rough in others. While there are other routes to Yellow Pine, none is more beautiful than the drive over Lick Creek Summit. However, motor homes over twenty feet and vehicles pulling trailers should not take this route. For an optional route see the trip to Stibnite, page 115.

Best time to travel

Weekdays, mid-June to late October offer the best opportunity to travel to Yellow Pine with the least amount of company. Prior to July 1, check with the Payette National Forest for road closures or restrictions.

Facilities

As a back country community, Yellow Pine offers most services. The Yellow Pine General Store has basic groceries and sundries, while the Yellow Pine Restaurant and Tavern serves ample meals and drinks. Visitors who want to spend a few days can find accommodations at the Yellow Pine Hotel and the Alpine Village. Cabins and RV spaces are also available.

Camping

Yellow Pine Campground, less than a mile from Yellow Pine, is located on Johnson Creek Road (FS413). Maintained by the

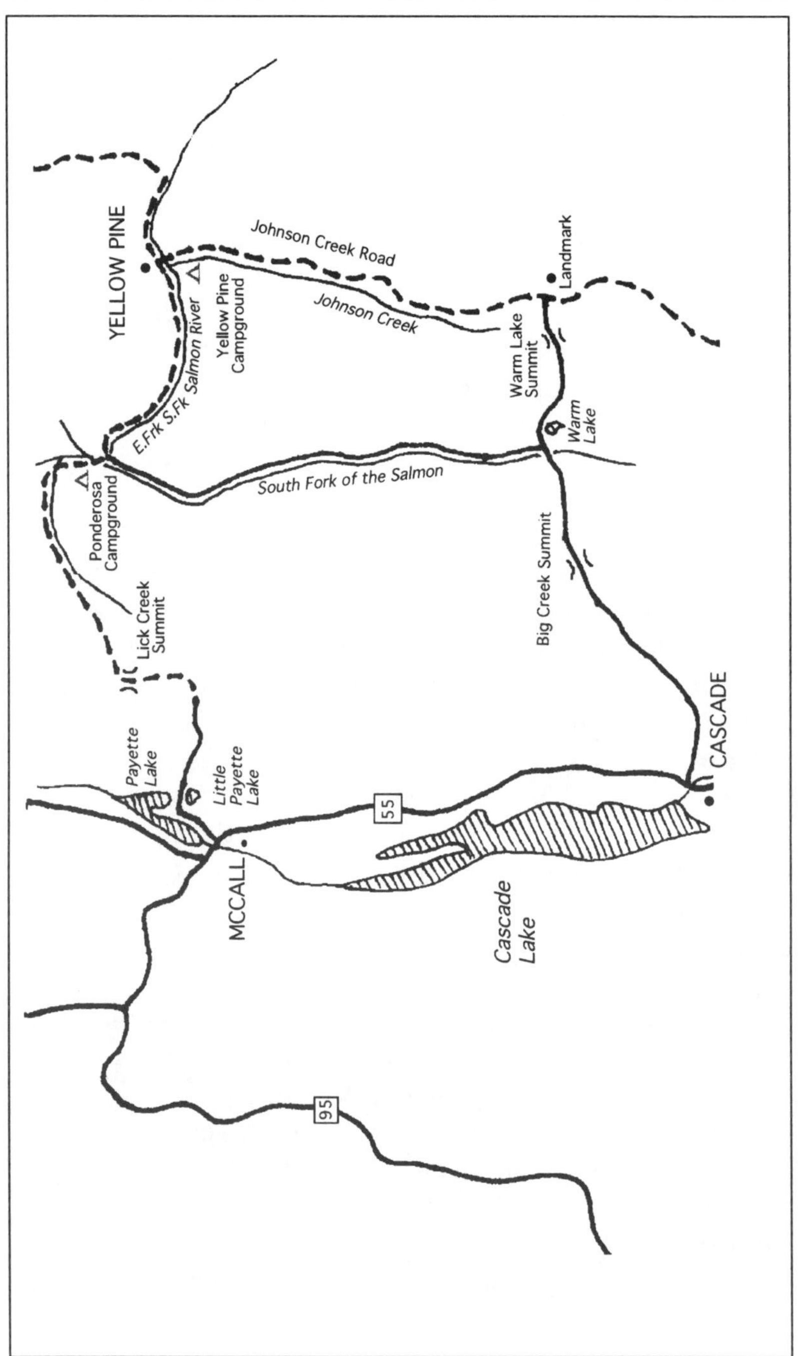
YELLOW PINE
Johnson Creek Road
Johnson Creek
Yellow Pine Campground
E.Frk S.Fk Salmon River
Landmark
Warm Lake Summit
Warm Lake
South Fork of the Salmon
Ponderosa Campground
Lick Creek Summit
Big Creek Summit
CASCADE
Payette Lake
Little Payette Lake
55
MCCALL
Cascade Lake
95

Forest Service, the campground features water and pit toilets.

Golden Gate Campground, another Forest Service campground, is located two miles south of Yellow Pine on Johnson Creek Road.

On the Way

Little Payette Lake

Lake Fork Campground—picnic and camping area, FS trail access, ten miles from McCall

Slick Rock—vertical granite formation, used by area rock climbers

Lick Creek Summit—elevation 6,789 feet

Ponderosa Campground—picnic and camping area, FS trail access, thirty-one miles northeast of McCall on the Secesh River

Chinese rock house—interpretive information

East Fork of the South Fork of the Salmon River

Caution

Lick Creek Road is a steep, one-lane road in places, especially on the east side of Lick Creek Summit. The road can also be extremely rough in mid-summer, with washboard sections. It is usually graded in late July in preparation for the Yellow Pine Harmonica Festival.

Getting there

In McCall, starting east on Railroad Street, follow the signs to Ponderosa State Park. Head north on Davis Street until you reach the intersection of Davis and Lick Creek Road. Turn right onto Lick Creek Road. After two miles, the road will come to a Y. Continue on Lick Creek Road and follow this road for another forty-five miles to Yellow Pine. The townsite is located one-quarter mile north of the main road. It is well-marked.

Miscellaneous Information

Yellow Pine is isolated and operates on its own easy-going timetable. Never count on a particular business to be open. It may be, but then again, the owners may have decided to go fishing. Also, make sure you have a full tank of gas before leaving McCall.

The Yellow Pine Harmonica Festival is nationally known.

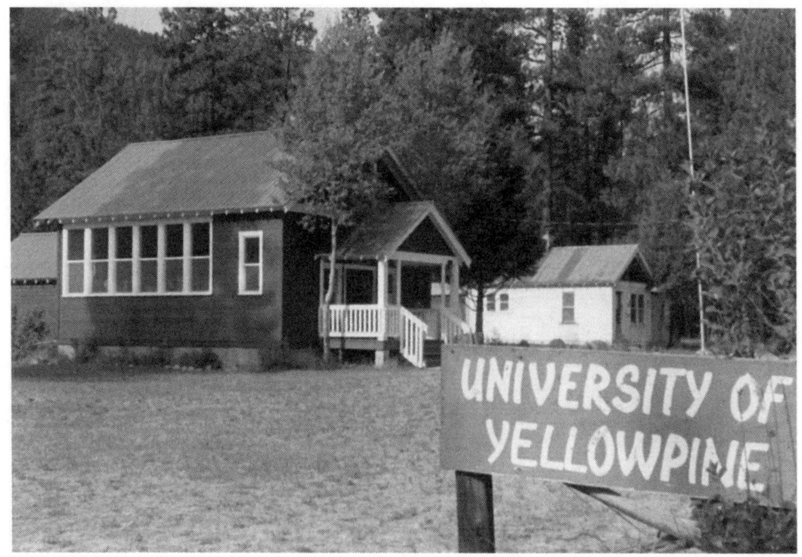

The Yellow Pine School House

Held the first weekend in August, the population of the community swells to over 1,000, and visitors are treated to back yard barbecues and great harmonica music.

History

Yellow Pine owes its existence to the miners of Central Idaho and the vision of Al Behne. Behne founded Yellow Pine in 1902 when he built a cabin on Johnson Creek, near the site of the present-day Yellow Pine cemetery. At that time, the area was simply known as Yellow Pine Basin.

When Behne's Johnson Creek cabin burned, he started over, moving to the site of present day Yellow Pine. With the gold rush to Thunder Mountain and the Big Creek area, the basin was a great stopping place for miners on their way to their claims. Eventually, Behne built a general store, and in 1906, opened the first post office in the area.

However, it was not until the discovery of gold and antimony on Meadow Creek, fourteen miles east of Yellow Pine, that the community began to grow. Mines like Cinnebar, Bonanza, Meadow Creek, and Yellow Pine brought miners into the area.

When the United Mercury Mine Company bought the Meadow Creek Claims in 1921, Yellow Pine was truly established.

Behne envisioned Yellow Pine as a modern community in Idaho's back country, complete with high rise buildings and paved streets. But Yellow Pine's isolation was too much to overcome.

The first wagon road into the area left Long Valley, near Cascade, and traveled past Warm Lake, then north over Cabin Creek summit before dropping into Johnson Creek to Yellow Pine. In the summer, it took travelers three days to make the trip. In 1917, a road was built over Warm Lake summit to Landmark and down Johnson Creek to Yellow Pine. During peak mining operations in the late 1920s and 1940s, this was the preferred route. It was even kept open in the winters from 1941 to 1953.

In 1952, work began on a road from Yellow Pine, west down the East Fork of the South Fork, opening up a shorter route to McCall over Lick Creek Summit. At the same time, construction started on a road from Warm Lake following the South Fork of the Salmon River. Over the years, the maintenance of both of these routes has caused controversy and frustration.

With the transportation problems, Yellow Pine could not produce the prosperity Behne envisioned. Thus, its fortunes rose and fell with those of the mining operations in the area. Still, the small community of Yellow Pine and a few hearty residents managed to survive.

Yellow Pine opened its first school, grades one through eight, in 1920 with eight children in attendance. The teacher, Miss Smith, held class in a tent. When one of the students appeared at school wrapped in a bear hide, Smith quit, and school was canceled for the remainder of the year. School resumed in the fall of 1921 with a male teacher from Harvard.

Eventually, the people of Yellow Pine built a one room school house with an adjoining woodshed. Wood was used to heat the school until 1967, when an oil heater was installed, and the woodshed was turned into a recreation room. Teachers were paid $75 a month with an additional $5 a month for janitorial duties.

Enrollment peaked in 1941, with twenty-seven students. The community supported the school until 1961, when McCall-Donnelly School District took over operations. Over the years, it closed sporadically due to lack of students. It operated last in 2000.

Electricity came to Yellow Pine in 1963, after the Civil Defense Agency declared it was eligible for emergency disaster funds. Families in the community, thirty-two in all, gave $100.00 each to help fund a diesel-powered electrical plant, which gave people power from 7 a.m. until 10 p.m. Residents of Yellow Pine maintained the generators. Presently, Idaho Power takes care of the community's electrical needs.

Visitors who choose to visit Yellow Pine will not only get a glimpse into an Idaho back-country community, but will also experience some of the best scenery Idaho has to offer.

For More Information

Payette National Forest
McCall Ranger District
102 W. Lake Street
McCall, Idaho 83638
(208) 634-0400

Yellow Pine Harmonica Contest
P.O. Box 30
Yellow Pine, Idaho 83677
(208) 633-3300
www.harmonicacontest.com

Yellow Pine General Store
(208) 633-3300

Yellow Pine Hotel
(208) 633-3377

Alpine Village
Yellow Pine, Idaho 83677
(208) 385-0271

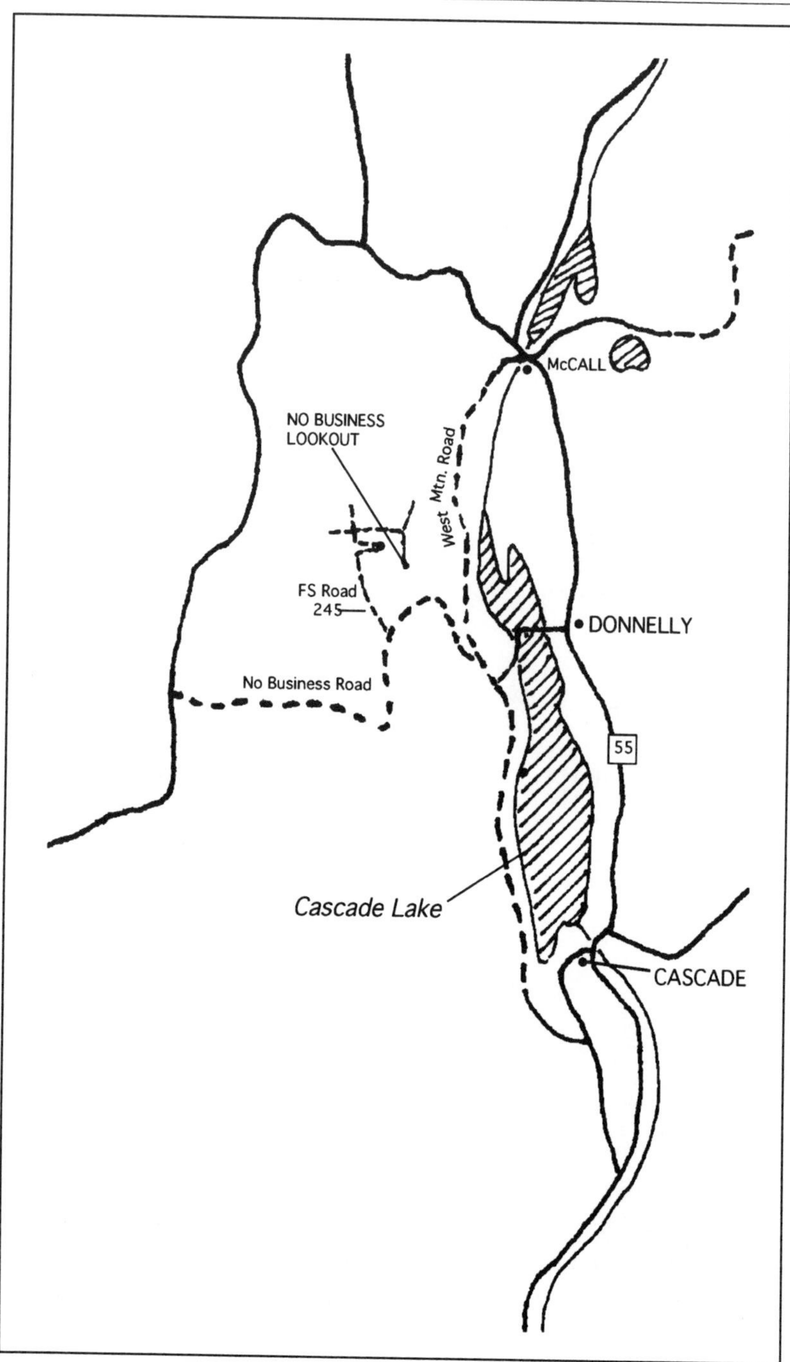
McCALL
NO BUSINESS
LOOKOUT
West Mtn. Road
FS Road
245
DONNELLY
No Business Road
55
Cascade Lake
CASCADE

No Business Lookout

Description

At 7,330 feet, No Business Lookout stands watch over the entire area. A trip to the lookout will give you a feel for the layout of McCall and the surrounding lakes, valleys, and mountains.

Distance/Direction/Conditions

Located southwest of McCall, No Business Lookout is a sixty-one mile round trip. The road varies from state highway and paved county road, to improved gravel and one lane mountain road. The last few miles to the lookout are bumpy and narrow, making this route unsuitable for recreational vehicles or vehicles pulling trailers. As with all back-country roads, this one can be dusty as well.

Best Time to Travel

The lookout is open mid-June to October, depending on snowpack. Try to go when the lookout is occupied, as you can learn much more about No Business and the area from the person who works there. The Southern Idaho Timber Protective Association (SITPA), located on Deinhard Lane, would have this information.

Facilities

No facilities are available.

Camping

The state operates several campgrounds around Lake Cascade, but none are on the way to the lookout.

On the way

Donnelly has several restaurants and a convenience store where you can pick up drinks and snacks for the trip.

The rest area at the corner of Tamarack Falls and West Mountain Roads is a good place to stop, as shortly after it, the pavement ends, and you begin your climb up the mountain. Pit toilets and water are available. Picnic tables are available at the site.

No Business Saddle sits at an elevation of 5,820 feet. At this point you will begin a descent that will take you to the road that leads to the lookout.

Caution

While the road is in good condition, it can be a washboard. Drive slowly in these areas. Also keep an eye out for deer.

On the return trip to McCall, you follow West Mountain Road, which is open range country. Be alert for cattle and sheep on the road.

Getting There

From the south end of McCall, head south on Highway 55 to Donnelly, eleven miles. In Donnelly, turn right (west) on West Roseberry Road. This road will take several turns. At Mile 11.5, follow the road left onto Norwood Road. Then at Mile 12.5 turn right onto Tamarack Falls Road, which will lead to West Mountain Road.

Turn right on West Mountain Road; soon the pavement will end. After one mile on this dirt road, begin looking for No Business Road, which will be on your left. Take this road up the mountain. You will pass No Business Saddle and head down the west side of the mountain.

At Mile 22.5, turn right. A sign there will indicate the distance to Squaw Flat and No Business Lookout. The road will wander up the west side of the mountain towards the lookout.

At Mile 27.6, the road will fork. Take the road to the right that indicates the lookout is three miles away and continue for 1.5 miles; then turn right again. At this point you will see the power lines that head to the lookout. Follow this road and the signs to the lookout.

For the return trip, retrace your route to West Mountain Road. There, turn left (north) and follow the road back to McCall. You will make stops at Wisdom Road, turn left, and at Boydstun Street; turn left again. This will take you back to Highway 55 on

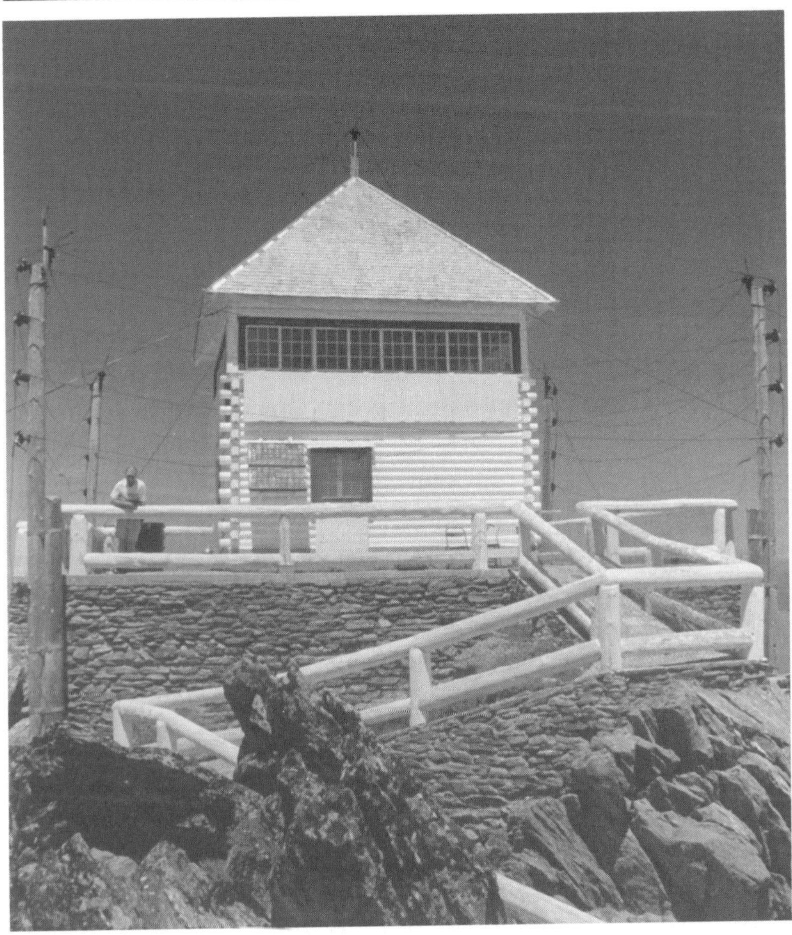

No Business Lookout

the west end of McCall.

Miscellaneous information

While the lookout is open to the public, it is also someone's private summer home. You need permission to enter.

History

When most people think of forest fire protection, the Forest Service usually comes to mind, but in Central Idaho, the Southern Idaho Timber Protective Association (SITPA) was the first organization established to protect the forests. No Business Lookout is an integral part of that protection.

Although its name was not formalized until 1919, SITPA was organized in 1904 as a cooperative among four private timber companies. Its purpose was to provide fire protection for their timberlands. The companies–Boise Lumber, Barber Lumber, A.W.Cook Timber, and Payette Lumber and Manufacturing–used their loggers and mill workers to fight forest fires.

Soon after, the state of Idaho and the Payette and Boise National Forests joined forces with SITPA, along with other lumber businesses. By 1929, in addition to the state and federal alliance, the association had fifty-four members and protected over a million acres of forest land in seven Idaho counties. Today, SITPA protects a little over 400,000 acres of private and state land in Valley, Adams, and Idaho counties in addition to 132,000 acres of federal lands in Valley and Adams counties.

To watch over the expansive forests in the area, SITPA built seven lookouts on some of the higher peaks around the valley. While the exact construction dates have been lost, the lookouts existed as early as 1914. The present structure at No Business was built around 1937 under the direction of two Finnish carpenters from McCall, using the manpower of the Civilian Conservation Corps. The lookout underwent renovations in the 1980s, including new concrete stem walls, but much of the original log work is intact.

No Business is one of two lookouts still operated by SITPA. The other is Brundage Mountain. Usually, they are occupied from July 1 to October 1, but the opening depends on the previous winter's snow pack. During dry years, they can open as early as the second week of June.

Those working on the lookout have one major task: to spot fires early when they are still manageable for fire fighters. Lookout personnel work five days a week, and while an official work day runs from 10 a.m. to 7 p.m., most will tell you that "when you're awake, you're looking."

No Business provides most of the comforts of home. The two-storied structure features living quarters on the main floor while the work area, complete with maps, communication equipment, and a 360 degree view, is on the the second floor. However, the site lacks running water; water has to be packed in, and the bathroom is a well-built outhouse perched on the edge of the mountain.

Thunderstorms offer special circumstances. No matter what the hour, lookout personnel are up and looking when a storm blows through, as most fires in the forest are lightening caused. In addition, all electrical appliances must be unplugged and all windows closed tightly as the lookout is a ready target for a damaging thunderbolt. Solid copper wires, all grounded, surround the structure for protection, but still the lightening can wreak havoc. In 1992, a lightening strike hit No Business and took out all the radio equipment.

In addition to watching for fire, lookout personnel serve another purpose: educating the public. Between 600-800 people visit No Business Lookout each year. SITPA uses this opportunity to teach those visitors about fire prevention. Visitors are always welcome, and those manning the lookout are knowledgeable not only about fire prevention, but also about the area's history as well.

The view from the lookout and the lessons learned make a trip to No Business well worth the time and effort.

For More Information

Southern Idaho Timber Protective Association
555 Deinhard Lane
McCall, Idaho 83638
(208) 634-2268

Payette National Forest
McCall Ranger District
P.O. Box 1062
102 W. Lake Street
McCall, Idaho 83638
(208) 634-0400

South Fork Road

Description

If you can take only one scenic drive during your stay, it must be the South Fork Road. The 118 mile round trip follows one of Idaho's most rugged and picturesque rivers, the South Fork of the Salmon.

Distance/Direction/Conditions

This route makes a loop that leads south to Cascade, then east to Warm Lake, before heading north down the South Fork. You follow two-lane state highways for 50 miles, before reaching a one lane paved road that follows the river. The last thirty-six miles can be rough as you follow Lick Creek Road back to McCall.

Best Time to Travel

If you can take this route on a weekday, you will have the road mostly to yourself; weekends, however, will be crowded.

The first eighty-two miles of this road are open year round, although winter conditions can make the road treacherous. The entire route is open from late June until mid-October, but you should always contact the Payette National Forest if you plan to go in late June. Many travelers have found their way blocked by huge snow drifts on Lick Creek Summit as late as July 4.

Facilities

None—this is just a scenic drive.

Camping

The Forest Service has numerous campground and picnic spots along the river. It has also erected interpretive signs at many of the campgrounds to inform visitors about the wildlife, the fishing, and the history of the area.

Campgrounds include the South Fork, Mile 49.8; Poverty Flats, Mile 65; Camp Creek, Mile 71.4; Buckhorn Bar, Mile 75.6; and Ponderosa, Mile 87.8. In the summer these campgrounds

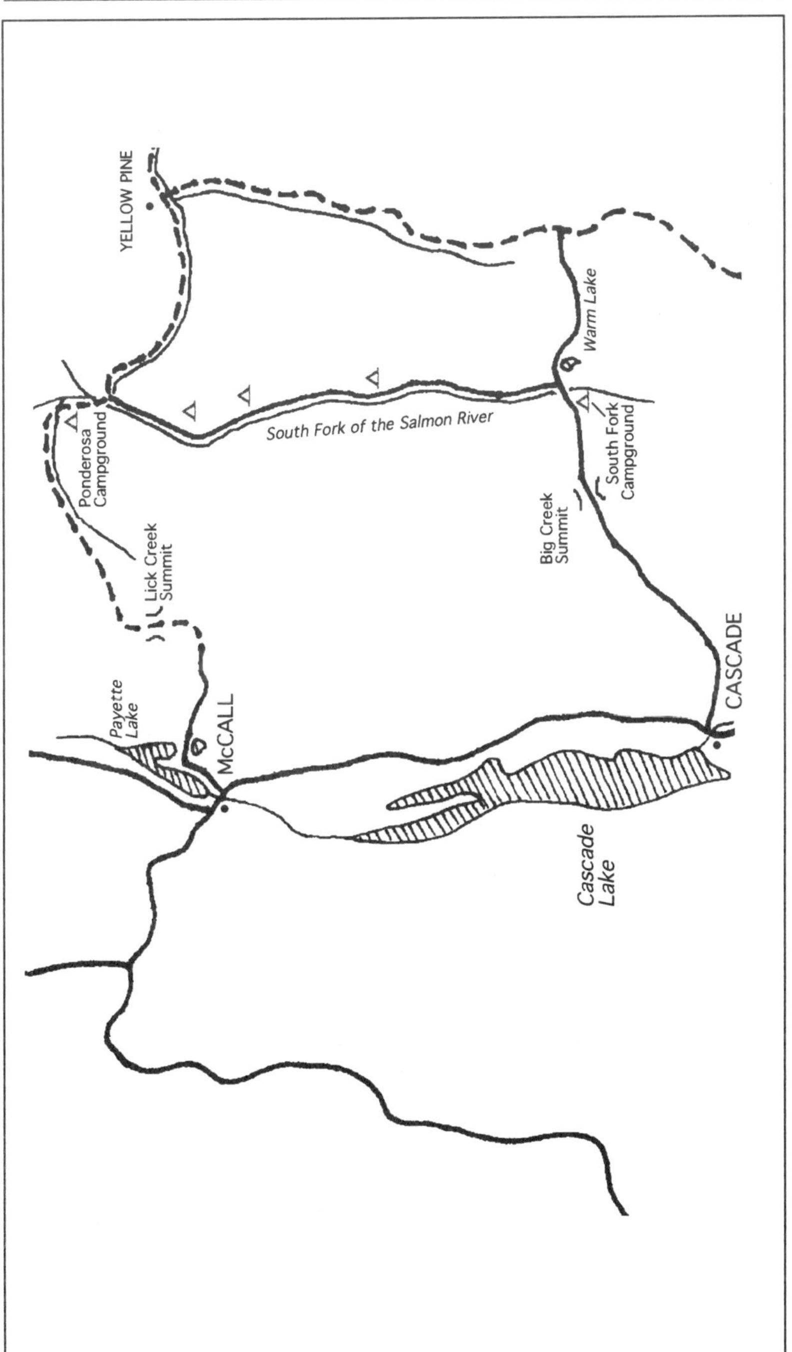
YELLOW PINE
Warm Lake
South Fork of the Salmon River
Ponderosa Campground
South Fork Campground
Lick Creek Summit
Big Creek Summit
Payette Lake
McCALL
CASCADE
Cascade Lake

Chinese rock house on the South Fork of the Salmon

include water, picnic tables, fire rings, and pit toilets.

On the Way

Donnelly is the only community directly on the route. Here you can pick up cold drinks and snacks.

Big Creek Summit—elevation 6,549 feet

Molly's Hot Springs—1.5 miles off the main road, at Mile 50.1 on the road to Stolle Meadows—is a unique site; bathtubs have been set up alongside the river. Hoses carry the clean, very hot water (114F) to the tubs.

Knox, the original settlement at Warm Lake, is at Mile 60 (see page 13). Many of the old buildings are still standing, and elk and moose can often be seen in the meadow.

Krassel Ranger Station is part of the Payette National Forest. A work crew is stationed here throughout the summer. The buildings were constructed in 1939 by the CCC, who also built an airstrip on the bench above the ranger station. The buildings are listed on the National Register of Historic Places.

A Chinese rock house, at Mile 83, sits on the east side of the river. The Forest Service restored the house, and interpretive signs next to the road explain the Chinese presence in the area.

Lick Creek summit—elevation 6,879 feet

Caution

Don't be misled by the paved road that follows the South Fork. This winding, narrow road has hairpin turns; when the signs read 10 mph, follow the recommendation and slow down. Also, it is one lane, so always be ready to take a turn-out when you see oncoming traffic. While this drive is beautiful in the fall, it is also a prime hunting area for deer and elk. Be ready for traffic and wear brightly colored clothes if you venture away from your car.

Getting There

From McCall, head south on Highway 55, through Donnelly and on to the north end of Cascade. Prior to entering Cascade, the Warm Lake Road will take off to the left (east). Take this road and follow it as it climbs up and over Big Creek Summit. At Mile 50.5, pay attention as the South Fork Road will come in on your left. Turn left here on to Forest Road 474. This road will follow the South Fork of the Salmon River for the next thirty-two miles and pass various Forest Service campgrounds. At Mile 82.5, the road will meet Lick Creek Road. A turn right (east) will take you to Yellow Pine. You will turn left (west) and travel the thirty-six miles back to McCall over Lick Creek Summit.

Miscellaneous

The South Fork is a prime spawning ground for Chinook salmon who make their way up the Columbia River each spring and summer from the Pacific Ocean. At one time, fifty-five percent of the fish from this run came from the South Fork. However, this fishery was nearly destroyed in the 1950s and '60s by excessive logging which led to erosion that clogged the river with sediment. Concentrated efforts by various government and environmental groups have led to increased fish runs in the past several years. While the runs will never equal those of the past, the return of the salmon gives credence to the power of nature and its creatures. If you take this route in the late summer, you can see the fish building their nests in shallow, slow-moving sections of the river. Be sure not to disturb the fish or the nests.

History

The South Fork's history echoes that of all Idaho rivers. Settlers traveled its banks in search of gold, found little, and ended up establishing homesteads on the bars at the river's edge. They eked out livings the best they could, but life was hard and isolated. Only the hardiest of souls could live for any length of time in this rugged part of Idaho.

Although substantial gold strikes were made in various locations in Central Idaho leading to rapid settlement, the South Fork was virtually untouched. Miners traveling to Thunder Mountain mining camps from the Treasure Valley traveled as far as Knox, then cut over the mountains to Johnson Creek, rather than travel down the South Fork. Miners from Warren on the way to Thunder Mountain crossed the South Fork then climbed Elk Summit to Big Creek to the gold mines there and beyond. While there were some grandiose plans to mine up and down the South Fork, no real community was ever established. Instead, the early settlers on the South Fork established homesteads and then did what they could to survive.

Among these were Jim Rains, killed on his ranch in 1879 by the Sheepeater Indians, and Sylvester "Three-Finger" Smith, who nearly lost his life in a battle with the Sheepeaters in Long Valley. Others dealt with tragedy of another kind, such as Harry Fritzer, whose wife died at thirty-four, shortly after giving birth to their eleventh child. The Fritzer family still holds the original homestead. Many of those living on the South Fork were colorful, if not notorious, including George Krassel, a German immigrant, who was shot and killed by William "Deadshot" Reed, supposedly in an argument concerning World War I.

These early settlers made their way to the river by trail, especially on the upper end of the South Fork. The first road established on this south end did not follow the South Fork at all. Instead it ran from Knox over the mountains to Nickel Creek. It was not until 1952 that people living in the back country of Yellow Pine and Stibnite realized that a road down the South Fork would make for easier traveling to their isolated communities.

Thus, in 1952, a road was built from Yellow Pine down the East Fork of the South Fork of the Salmon River. At the same time, the Forest Service began work on a road from Warm Lake down the South Fork, eight miles to Goat Creek. The plan was eventually to connect these two roads. But the plan ran into trouble. In 1964, heavy snows led to major slides and washouts and caused the Forest Service to abandon the project. The road was left to the elements and eroded into the river, causing major damage to the salmon habitat. It started a controversy that rages to this day.

In 1992, work began to rebuild the road. In 1994, with the help of eight million dollars of federal funds, the South Fork Road was completed. Today, Forest Service crews continually work to maintain the road, which is plowed in the winter to give residents of Yellow Pine access to the rest of the world. It is also this route that gives visitors to Central Idaho a glimpse of one of the state's most spectacular rivers.

For More Information

Krassel Ranger District
Payette National Forest
500 N. Mission St.
McCall, Idaho 83638
(208) 634-0600

McCall Ranger District
Payette National Forest
102 W. Lake Street
McCall, Idaho 83638
(208) 634-0400

Cascade Ranger District
Boise National Forest
P.O. Box 696
Cascade, Idaho 83611
(208) 382-4271

Council/Fruitvale

Description

This trip takes you on a back-road loop to Council, Idaho over the No Business Saddle.

Distance/Direction/Road Conditions

Council, by back roads, is forty-seven miles from McCall. The return trip, following Highway 95 is shorter, making the total trip eighty-two miles. The roads are usually in good shape, with improved gravel roads for fifty miles and the rest pavement. Expect some washboard sections on the gravel road.

Best Time to Travel

This route to Council is not heavily traveled and makes a good trip anytime. The road is usually open from mid-June to mid-November, depending on snowfall.

Facilities

A typical Idaho community, Council features restaurants, gas stations, a convenience store on each of end of town, and a nine-hole golf course.

Camping

Several camping and picnic spots are available along the way, including Council's City Park.

Cabin Creek Campground, with campsites, fire rings, and pit toilets, is located thirty-one miles into the trip. Evergreen Campground, off Highway 95, is located between Council and New Meadows on the return trip home. It features picnic tables and pit toilets.

On the Way

Donnelly offers a delectable bakery, restaurants, and a convenience store.This is the last place to stock up on snacks and drinks before heading over the mountain.

A rest area is available at the corner of Tamarack Falls and West Mountain Roads.

White Licks Hot Springs at Mile 23.6 is on private land, but

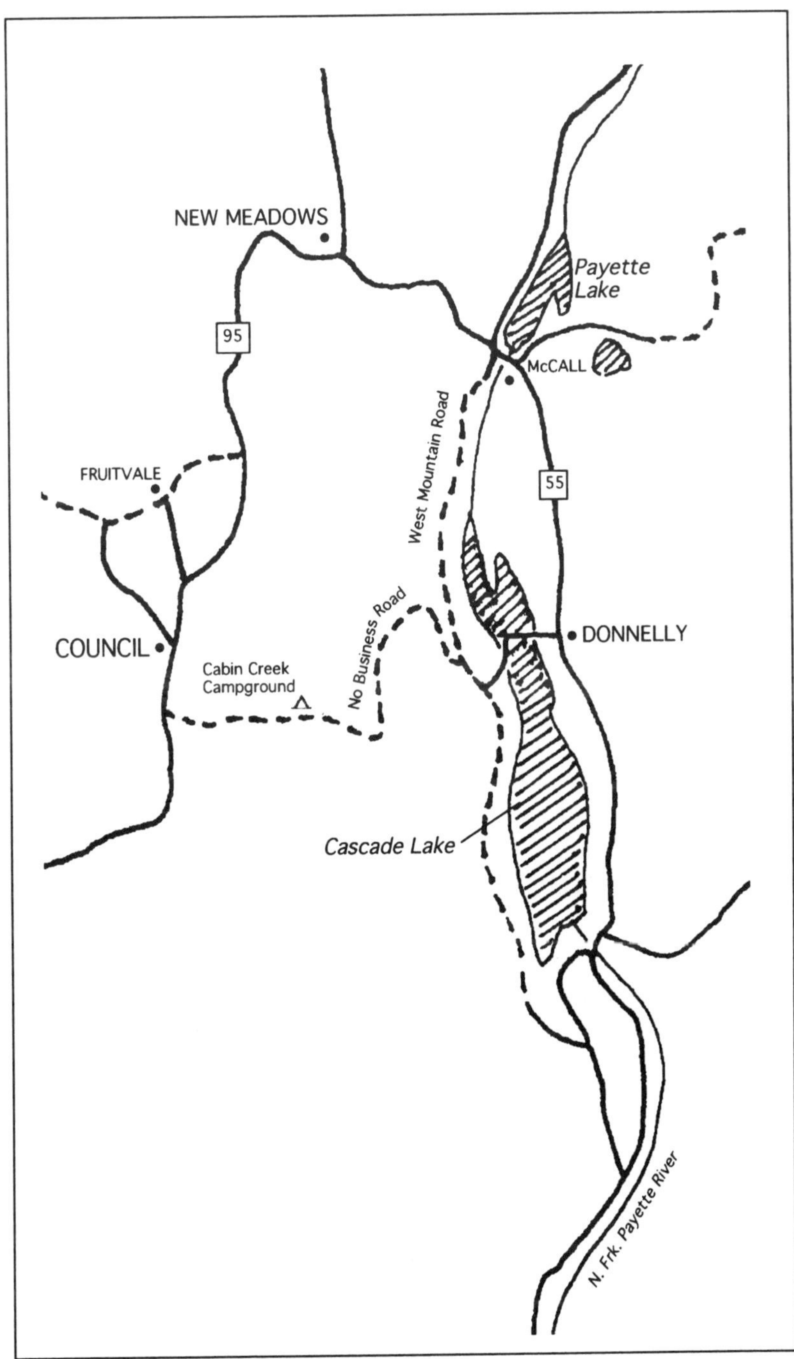
NEW MEADOWS
Payette Lake
95
McCALL
West Mountain Road
55
FRUITVALE
No Business Road
DONNELLY
COUNCIL
Cabin Creek Campground
Cascade Lake
N. Frk. Payette River

is used by the public. The naturally hot water is diverted into three small bathhouses. No restroom facilities are available.

Caution

The route over No Business Lookout is heavily populated with deer. Also, as a back-country road, it can be a washboard, so pay particular attention on sharp corners. Also, the community of Donnelly has a posted, strictly enforced, speed limit of twenty-five miles per hour.

Getting There

From McCall, head south on Highway 55 to Donnelly. Once in Donnelly, turn right (west) onto West Roseberry Road. It winds its way east, then south, then east again, changing names to Norwood Road, then Tamarack Falls Road. Follow Tamarack Falls Road until it intersects West Mountain Road. Turn right on West Mountain Road. The pavement will soon end. Continue approximately one mile on West Mountain Road. At Mile 13.5, No Business Road will take off on your left. Turn on to this road.

The road will head up the mountain and pass through No Business Saddle. You will then begin a meandering descent, passing the turn off to No Business Lookout (see page 50), White Licks Hot Springs and Cabin Creek Campground. At Mile 42, you will reach Highway 95. Turn right (north) to Council.

Once in Council, continue to follow Highway 95 north. At Mile 51.6, the main highway will veer right. You continue straight, following the road to Fruitvale; make sure you check for oncoming traffic. This is not a free pass.

After two miles, the pavement ends. Continue following the main road. Check out the railroad trestles and the old railroad line, now a bike trail that runs from Tamarack to Council. At Mile 56.7, you will see an assortment of buildings on your left. This was once known as Starkey, a popular hot springs resort, now closed to the public. Continue on this county road. At mile 61, you return to Highway 95. Turn left (north) and travel to New Meadows. Once in New Meadows, take Highway 55 back to McCall.

The bathhouses at White Licks Hot Springs

Miscellaneous

As with all small towns, Council has its share of celebrations. One that shouldn't be missed is the Council Mountain Festival. Held each year on the Fourth of July, the festival features the World Championship Porcupine Race.

History

Council owes its name to several Indian tribes who regularly gathered in the valley, up until about 1872. The tribes—Nez Perce, Coeur d'Alene, Sheepeater, Lemhi, Umatilla, Klikitat, Shoshone, and Bannock—met to trade, fish, and take part in competitive games.

With the discovery of gold in Florence and Warren in the early 1860s, a principle route for pack trains developed following the Weiser River through the Council Valley north to Meadows Valley and beyond. However it wasn't until the 1870s that the first settlers decided to make the Council Valley their home.

The first homesteaders, George and Elizabeth Moser, arrived in 1876; the present Moser Avenue was the site of their first cabin. Eventually, they built a larger, two story house and served as hosts to travelers heading to the mining areas of Seven Devils or Warren. They raised cows, cattle, and pigs and sold milk, butter, and meat to the miners.

Others followed the Mosers to the valley. Two families arrived in 1877 with several more coming in 1878. Originally the community was called Hornet, as the fledgling town sat at the confluence of Hornet Creek and the Weiser River. It also went by the name of Buckshot, the nickname of George Moser. In 1877, settlers met to name their community officially. The majority wanted to call it Moser Valley, but Moser objected. Eventually they settled on "Council Valley" and with the establishment of a post office in 1878, it became official.

By 1885, 300 people were living in Council Valley. The loosely formed community featured an inn, a blacksmith shop, and two saloons. The first school was built in 1879 and a second was added in 1885. The first mercantile appeared in 1888. Buildings and homesteads stretched the entire length of the valley, with no real community center.

That changed in the 1890s when the Mosers began selling pieces of their homestead. Soon others followed and a town was born. Council was incorporated in January 1903. By December of 1905, Council's population had risen to 1,000. It boasted a hotel, a bakery, a newspaper, two millinery stores, three saw mills, three restaurants, three livery stables, three blacksmith shops, and six general stores. It was home to professionals as well, with a jeweler, a physician, and two lawyers. One Idaho magazine predicted Council would see sustained growth and reach a population of 5,000.

The Seven Devils boom in the early 1900s helped Council. The streets were filled with those affiliated with the mines from freighters to miners to investors. To meet lodging needs, the Pomona Hotel was built. Completed in 1910, the three story building featured nineteen sleeping rooms, a billiard room, and a formal dining room. Still standing, the building is on the National Register of Historic Places.

Council's economy also got a boost from the Mesa Orchards

Company, which established one of the largest orchards in the country. Located seven miles south of Council, over 1200 acres were cultivated in fruit trees, mostly apples. Evidence of the trees and the elaborate irrigation system can still be seen today.

In 1915, a devastating fire destroyed much of the commercial district of Council. Thus, the city leaders passed an ordinance requiring the use of brick in all new construction. Many of the brick buildings on Council's main street were built shortly thereafter.

After the mining bust of the Seven Devils, Council struggled to find its identity. Eventually ranching and logging became its livelihood, especially in 1939 with the construction of the Boise-Payette Mill. Eventually, it would become the largest employer in the community.

For over fifty years, the mill and the surrounding forest land made Council a thriving community. But when the timber industry began to decline, so did the fortunes of Council. When the mill closed in 1995, Council's future looked bleak. Still, the little town refuses to die. Council's civic leaders continue to promote the area as a great place to live and a nice place to visit. Residents boast of mild winters and long growing seasons, making the area a paradise in Idaho's mountains.

For More Information

Council Chamber of Commerce
Council, Idaho 83612
(208) 253-4851

Council Ranger District
Payette National Forest
500 E. Whitley
Council, Idaho 83612
(208) 253-0100

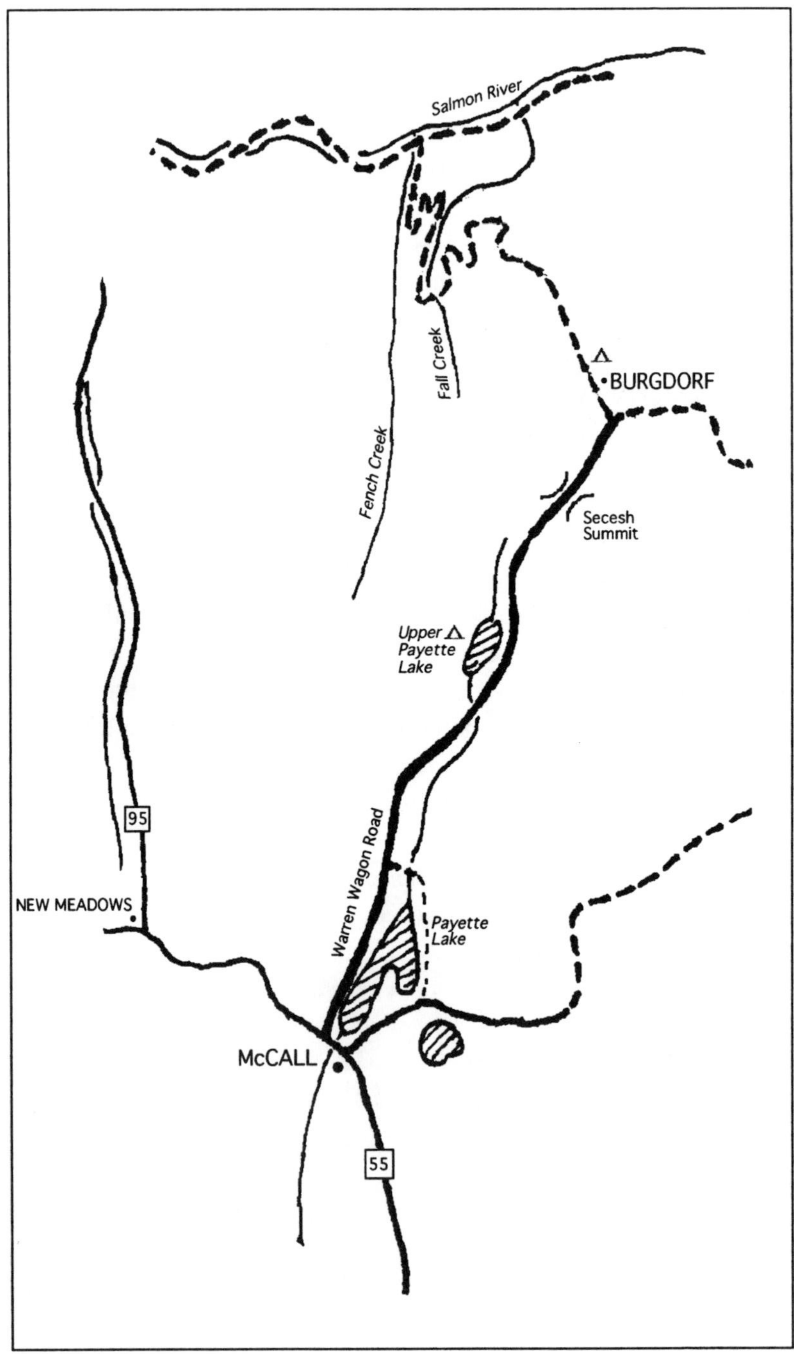
Salmon River
Fall Creek
BURGDORF
Fench Creek
Secesh
Summit
Upper
Payette
Lake
95
NEW MEADOWS
Warren Wagon Road
Payette
Lake
McCALL
55

Burgdorf

Description

Burgdorf is a natural hot springs used by miners and travelers as early as 1861. This drive features scenery, history, and an outdoor pool open to visitors.

Distance/Direction/Road Conditions

The drive to Burgdorf is easy, only thirty miles northeast of McCall with pavement for twenty-eight miles and an improved gravel road for two miles.

Best Time to Travel

The road to Burgdorf is open to automobile traffic from mid-May to late October, as heavy snows make the road impassable during the winter. The hot springs pool is a popular attraction, so you should avoid the weekends if possible. The best months to travel are May and early June, when the meadows are filled with elk and an occasional moose, and late September when the fall colors are the best in the area.

Facilities

The hot springs is open to the public. There is a minimal charge for adults and school aged children, but kids four and under can swim for free. Changing rooms are available as part of the fee.

Visitors who wish to spend the evening can also rent cabins by the day. The cabins are very rustic with wood stoves, kerosene lamps, and outhouses. Renters must bring their own food, bedding, and utensils.

Burgdorf also features a store that offers limited snacks and drinks. Visitors should always call ahead for up-to-date information.

Camping

No private camping is allowed at the hot springs. The Forest Service has several campgrounds in the vicinity. The Burgdorf

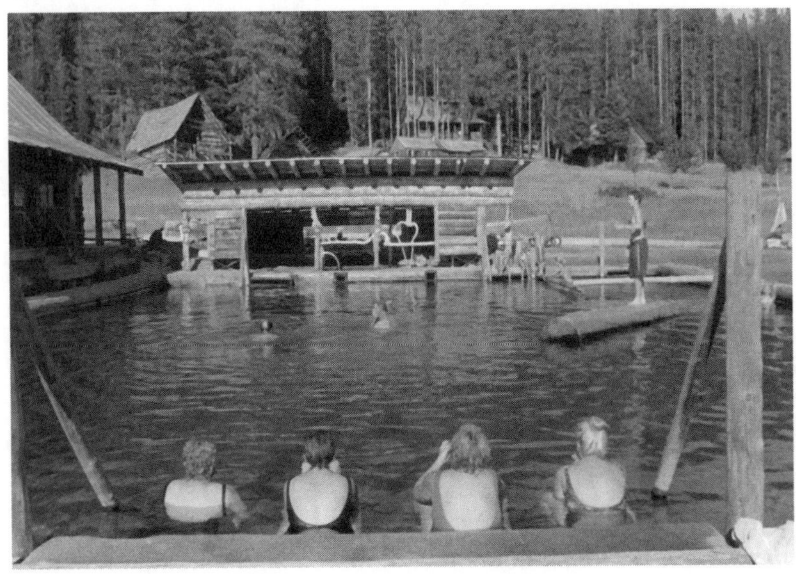

Enjoying the pool at Burgdorf

Campground is located just north of the hot springs and features picnic tables, fire grates, and pit-toilets

On the Way

Upper Payette Lake—picnic area, camping, fishing
Secesh Summit—heart of the 1994 Idaho wildfires
Secesh River—the last native Chinook Salmon run in Idaho

Caution

Watch out for deer on the road, any time of the year.

Getting There

From the west end of McCall, head northeast on Warren Wagon Road for twenty-eight miles. Immediately after crossing Lake Creek, the headwaters of the Secesh River, the pavement ends. Here Forest Road 246 comes in from the left. Turn left (north) on FS246, an improved dirt road, and follow the road for two miles. Burgdorf is situated on the east side of the road, and you will actually pass it before you come to the entrance, a sharp right turn. Follow the entryway to the parking lot.

Miscellaneous information

The hot springs pool is 50' x 75' with a sandy bottom and log sides. It is five feet deep in most spots, except for the children's pool. A soaking area at the hot end of the pool is over 106 degrees Fahrenheit. The pool itself ranges in temperature from 98 to 104 degrees. Usually, the pool closes at 8 p.m. to day swimmers, but the hours vary. People who rent cabins may use the pool at any time.

History

The Idaho gold rush of the 1860s gave rise to Burgdorf. After gold was discovered in Florence in 1861, and then in Warren in 1862, the area was bustling with mining activity. The natural hot water of the springs was a welcome relief to the early miners of Central Idaho. The hot springs, originally called Warm Springs, was conveniently located on the trail from Florence to Warren. It served as a halfway point, with Florence located seventeen miles to the north and Warren, fourteen miles to the east.

The first known person to lay claim to the springs was Fred Burgdorf, a German immigrant, who made his way to Warren in 1864. While he began his life in Warren as a gold miner, when he heard of the natural hot springs, he realized its potential. While historians disagree on when he actually occupied the site—some say 1865; others say 1870—he made it official shortly after 1870 when he filed a 160 acre mining claim that included the hot springs and the surrounding meadows. In 1902, he was granted a homestead patent on the entire 160 acres.

Burgdorf's first action was to change the name of the place to "Resort." He established a business and served the miners on their way to the various diggings in the area. Eventually, he built a twenty-room hotel, several cabins, and a general store. By 1903, a post office had been established there. In addition to the resort, Burgdorf also had a substantial cattle operation, which he maintained until 1910, and he invested in mining claims on the South Fork of the Salmon River.

In the late 1800s, a young singer-actress, Jeanette Foronsard, passed through Resort on her way to Warren. Burgdorf was smitten, and the two were married. Together, they turned the

The old hotel at Burgdorf

place into a first-class resort. Jeanette insisted on using fine China for serving, and after formal dinners, she would entertain guests with song. It was Jeanette who insisted on changing the name of the springs to "Burgdorf," which became official in 1914 with the renaming of the post office.

Burgdorf's resort weathered both boom and bust of the golden era of Idaho. Between 1861 and 1890, miners used the springs as a stopover on trips from Florence to Warren. In 1879, the US Cavalry retreated to the springs after being surprised by the Sheepeater Indians on Big Creek, thirty-eight miles to the east. In 1889, the Idaho Territorial Legislature approved financing for a wagon road that led from Meadows Valley past Resort north across the Salmon River to Mount Idaho, near Grangeville. The road was completed in 1892, and in 1901 was declared a state highway. When the Thunder Mountain gold rush began in 1902, this became a main route for the miners in the area.

Fred and Jeanette Burgdorf remained at the hot springs until the 1920s, when Jeanette became ill. She died in Portland in 1923. In August of that year, Burgdorf sold his property to James

Harris of McCall. Harris continued to build Burgdorf's reputation as a popular resort. He expanded the pool to its present size, built a larger store with a filling station, and added fifteen cabins. Harris also was responsible for the large, two-story hotel that still stands at Burgdorf.

Bill Harris took over from his father in the late 1940s, but soon after, the popularity of the resort declined. People were no longer looking for a rustic, back-country experience. While Burgdorf has always been open to the public, beginning in the 1960s, the Harris family made a conscious decision to stop promoting the hot springs. Today it is relatively unchanged from the Burgdorf of the 1940s. In 1973, Burgdorf was added to the National Register of Historic Places.

For More Information

McCall Ranger District
Payette National Forest
P.O. Box 1062
102 W. Lake Street
McCall, Idaho 83638
(208) 634-0400

Burgdorf Hot Springs
Warren Wagon Road
McCall, Idaho 83638
(208) 636-3036

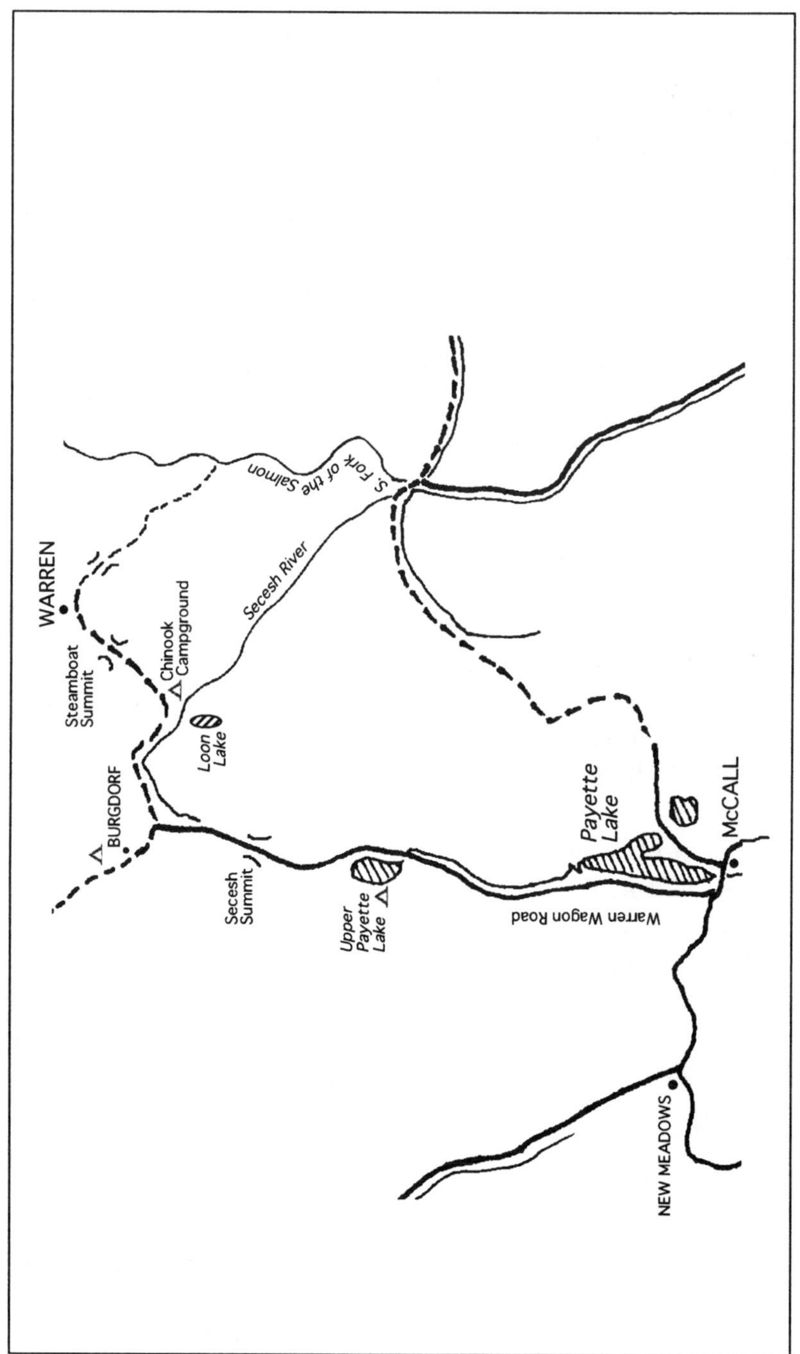
WARREN
Steamboat Summit
Chinook Campground
Secesh River
S. Fork of the Salmon
Loon Lake
BURGDORF
Secesh Summit
Upper Payette Lake
Payette Lake
McCALL
Warren Wagon Road
NEW MEADOWS

Warren

Description

With its main street featuring buildings over 100 years old, Warren will take you back to Idaho's glory days, when the cry of gold sent men scrambling in search of the mother lode. Evidence of mining is everywhere in Warren as is the rugged Idaho spirit. A visit to Warren is a great look at Idaho's earliest history.

Distance/Direction/Road Conditions

Located only forty-three miles northeast of McCall, it is an easy drive to Warren. The road is paved for twenty-eight miles while an improved dirt road takes you the final fifteen miles to the historic community. The dirt road, which can be rough in places, narrows as it follows the Secesh River, but there are numerous turnouts.

Best Time to Travel

The road is open mid-May to late October, depending on snowfall. The ever-changing scenery from spring to fall makes this a great trip. If you are planning a May or October excursion, however, contact the McCall Ranger District for road conditions.

Facilities

If you plan to have lunch or dinner in Warren, make sure to call ahead.

Secesh Stage Stop is located in Secesh Meadows, thirty-two miles from McCall. Food and beverages are available, as are rooms to rent. The hours vary, but the place is usually open seven days a week from early morning to early evening. Always call ahead to make sure, (208) 636-6798.

Winter Inn is located on the west end of Main Street in Warren. Food and drinks are available here, and Friday night's "Steak Night" is a hit with Warren regulars and visitors alike. The inn also has an interesting collection of mining artifacts and information on Warren's history. Hours vary, but the coffee is usually on by 11 a.m. The establishment usually stays open until the last customer leaves.

Backcountry Bed and Breakfast sits on the east end of Warren. Mountain decor and back-country hospitality are part of the experience. Visitors should call ahead for availability.

Camping

Chinook Campground, located at the east end of Secesh Meadows, is a beautiful campground right on the Secesh River. Camping sites and picnic tables are available. The trailheads for the Secesh River and Loon Lake are located here.

On the Way

Upper Payette Lake features several great picnic sites

Secesh Summit–elevation 6,424 feet

Secesh River–site of the last native Chinook salmon run in Idaho

Burgdorf is two miles out of the way, but a good side trip. See page 68 for details.

War Eagle Lookout gives you a view of the Salmon River and Lick Creek drainages and the Seven Devils. This is a steep, rutted road, often impassable. This should only be attempted with a high-clearance, four-wheel-drive vehicle.

Secesh Meadows was named by early miners who staked claims in the area in the 1860s, during the fury of the Civil War. The miners here favored secession.

Steamboat Summit–elevation 6,996 feet

Warren tailings–The mounds of rocks that seem to stretch forever in Warren were made by dredges working the area in the 1930s.

The Chinese Cemetery is located one-half mile west of Warren on the north side of the road. Parking is available, and a short trail leads to the cemetery.

Caution

Watch for deer on the road at any time. Also be cautious of truck traffic the final fifteen miles to Warren. Be prepared to use the turnouts.

If you decide to explore the area around Warren, avoid entering any mine shafts. While they may be inviting, they are also dangerous.

Getting There

From the northwest end of McCall, head north on Warren Wagon Road. You will follow the west shore of Payette Lake and the North Fork of the Payette River and pass Upper Payette Lake and Secesh Summit. At Mile 27, the pavement will end and you will come to an intersection. A left turn will take you to Burgdorf. Continue straight. You will follow the Secesh River for several miles and pass through Secesh Meadows. At approximately Mile 33, you will see the turnoff to Chinook Campground and begin your climb over Steamboat Summit. Continue on Warren Wagon Road over the summit and into the Warren Valley. At Mile 41 you will see the Warren dredge ponds, and at Mile 42 you will enter Warren.

Miscellaneous information

Warren is filled with rich Idaho history, well documented by the Payette National Forest. The Forest Service offers both an auto tour and a walking tour of Warren, both well worth your time. You can get more information from the McCall Ranger District Office located at 102 West Lake Street in McCall.

History

The fourth oldest mining community in the state, Warren is named after James Warren a shiftless, gambling prospector from Lewiston, Idaho, who led a group of miners into the area in August 1862. When they discovered gold on Warren Creek, word quickly spread and the rush was on. Within a year, over 2,000 miners worked placer claims in the area.

Warren originally was settled as two camps. The first, at the mouth of Slaughter Creek, on the east end of present day Warren, was started in September 1862, by miners loyal to the Confederacy; they named the community Richmond, in honor of the Confederate capital. Union sympathizers retaliated by congregating at the present Warren site; they called their camp Washington, as a symbol of their loyalty. However, no war between

Beargrass on Secesh Summit on the way to Warren

the camps transpired. When gold was discovered at the mouth of Slaughter Creek, Richmond was razed by placer miners who laid claim to the rich ground. With Richmond gone, miners settled in Washington, but its name, too, was short-lived. By 1877, the town was referred to most frequently as Warrens, a shortened version of Warren's Camp. Eventually, the name was shortened to Warren.

Population estimates during the early days in Warren vary. In 1865, an estimated 1,500 people lived in the area. They were served by two general stores, two saloons, a hotel, and a boarding house. Activity in the area was so great that in 1868, Warren was named the county seat of Idaho County, taking the place of once-prosperous Florence. It remained the county seat until 1875, when it gave way to Mt. Idaho, near present day Grangeville, 100 miles north of McCall.

Like all mining towns, Warren's fortunes waxed and waned. Early miners were very successful with their placer claims along

Warren Creek, but these deposits were soon depleted. In 1867, the first quartz mine was established and for the next several years, these hard rock mines provided much of the activity around Warren. But even these played out by the mid 1870s, giving way to an influx of Chinese miners.

The completion of the transcontinental railroad at Promontory Point, Utah, in 1869, left many Chinese immigrants without jobs. Many of them traveled north to Idaho in search of work, and by the mid-1870s, 1,200 of them lived in Warren. Initially, they were not allowed to file mining claims but eventually were allowed to purchase claims already worked by white miners. They also worked as cooks and servants for many of the families in the area. While they were subject to harsh treatment without any protection from the law, they survived by their industriousness and established their own community on the west end of Warren. Chinese businesses included a general store, a saloon, a gambling house, and a laundry. In 1882, five placer mining companies, owned by Chinese, were operating in Warren.

Many of the Chinese also made their way to the South Fork of the Salmon River, nine miles southeast of Warren, where the mild climate was perfect for gardening. Beginning in 1875, they built over 250 terraces on twenty-two acres. For over thirty-five years, the Chinese worked these gardens, selling their produce to the people in Warren and surrounding areas. Remnants of the terraces can still be seen. A strenuous, self-guided hiking tour through the terraces is available. Stop at the Warren Guard Station and ask for directions to the site, which is located on Forest Road #337.

Remnants of the Chinese Cemetery also can be found. Located at the west entrance to Warren, across from the Warren airfield, the cemetery appears on the National Register of Historic Places. The cemetery was used between 1870 and 1920, and archeological records show at least twenty-nine burial slots in the cemetery, although other sources list at least thirty-five interments at the site. This cemetery was only a temporary site for the Chinese; it was customary for them to make arrangements to be returned to their homeland for proper burial. Such was the case with the Warren Chinese Cemetery. Only one, but perhaps as many as three, remain buried in the cemetery. All others were exhumed and returned to China, the last one in the 1930s.

Eventually, the Chinese presence in Warren declined; by 1920 only a handful lived there. Ah Sam was one of the last Chinese survivors; he died in 1933 and is buried in the Warren Cemetery. In 1997 and 1999, Georgia Southern University sponsored a field school in Warren to study the Chinese who lived there. Chinese artifacts, collected in and around the area, can be seen at the Winter Inn and the Warren Guard Station.

The expanse of exposed river rock (tailings) that surrounds Warren hides the beauty of what once was a beautiful mountain valley. In 1904-1905, dredging began on Warren Creek and its tributaries. Powered by steam, the dredge with its huge buckets, tore up the stream beds, depositing the rock in its wake. The steam dredge suspended operation after only one year, but in 1932, two electric dredges were put to work. Over the next ten years, an estimated four million dollars in gold was taken from the Warren area. The tailings, damaged stream beds, and one of the dredges, now just scrap on Warren Creek, were left in its place.

Today, main street of Warren looks much as it did in the early 1900s. Isolated in Idaho's rugged back-country, it has been left virtually untouched, except for the effects of time. Inaccessible except by snowmobile from late October to mid-May, Warren has only eleven full time residents, many of whom know and appreciate Warren's colorful past. Much of this past can be imagined with a short walk to Warren's cemetery, established in 1863. While only a handful of the graves are marked, eighty-six people are buried in the hillside cemetery, located north of Warren's main street. While the trail to the cemetery is somewhat steep, it is worth the effort, as is the entire trip to Warren.

For More Information

McCall Ranger District
102 W. Lake Street
P.O. Box 1062
McCall, Idaho 83638
(208) 634-0400

Here you can obtain information on the Warren Auto and Walking Tour and a handout on the Chinese terraced gardens on the South Fork.

Winter Inn
Warren, Idaho 83671
(208) 636-4393

Warren Guard Station
Payette National Forest
Warren, Idaho 83671
(208) 636-8737

Secesh Stage Stop
Secesh Meadows
(208) 636-6798

Backcountry Bed and Breakfast
Warren, Idaho 83671
(208) 636-6000
email at backctry@ctcweb.net.

Monastery of St. Gertrude

Description

This trip takes you to a convent and remarkable museum located in the wheat fields of Camas Prairie. The Chapel of St. Gertrude is an architectural marvel, and the privately owned gallery is the most unique in the state. While it is a two-hour drive from McCall, it is well worth your time.

Distance/Direction/Road Conditions

The monastery is located 119 miles north of McCall, near the town of Cottonwood. With paved roads all the way, the round trip is easily accomplished in a day.

Best Time to Travel

Avoid Fridays and Sundays, as they are heavy travel days on Highway 95.

Facilities

The museum is open May through September, Tuesday-Saturday, 9:30 a.m.–4:30 p.m. and Sundays, 1:30–4:30 p.m. From October through April, the museum is open only Tuesday–Saturday.

Admission is $4.00 for adults and $1.00 for students. Children under six are free.

A picnic area and restrooms are available. Food, lodging, and gasoline can be found in nearby Cottonwood and Grangeville.

Camping

No camping accommodations are available.

On the Way

Two rest stops–Mile 38 and Mile 68

Riggins calls itself "The Whitewater Capital of the World." Take time to watch boaters shoot some of the rapids on the Salmon River as the road parallels the river for thirty miles.

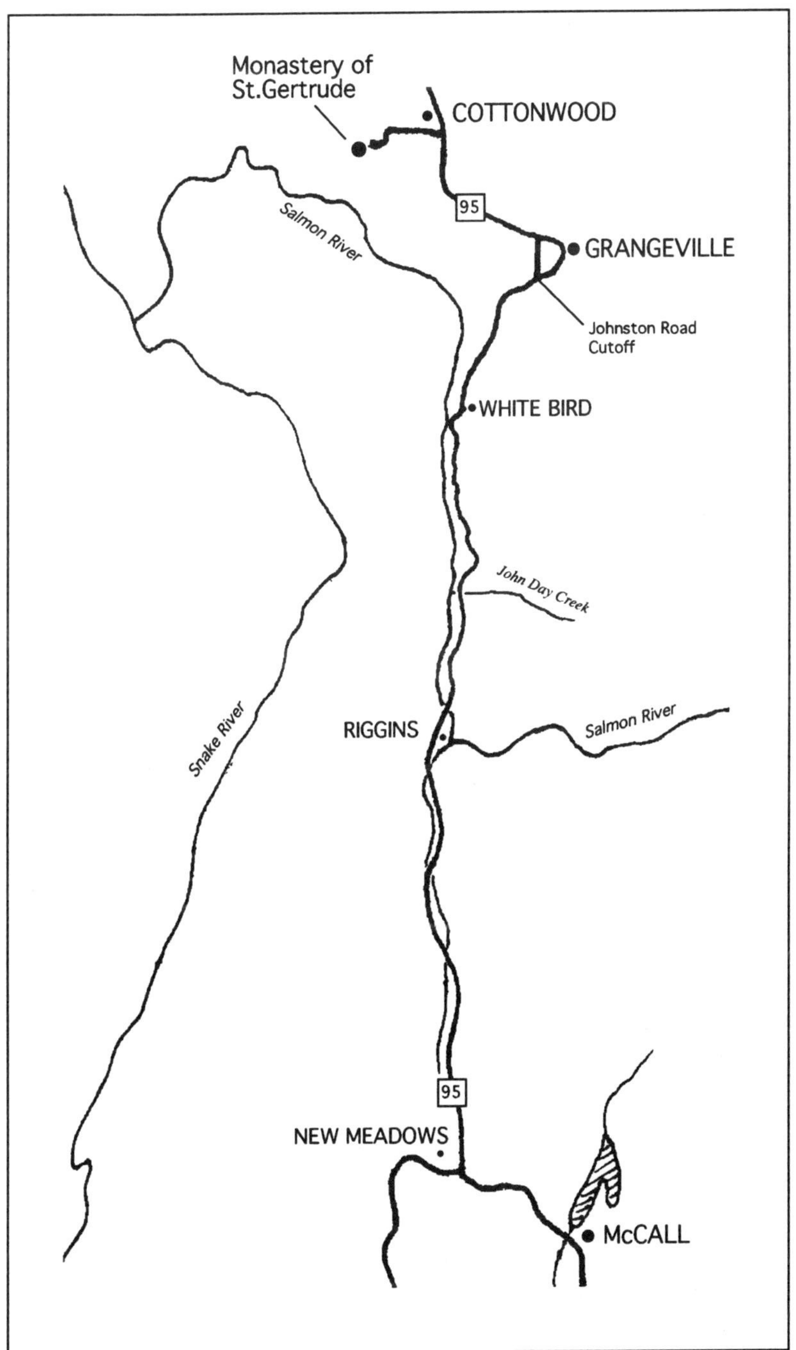
Monastery of
St.Gertrude
COTTONWOOD
95
GRANGEVILLE
Salmon River
Johnston Road
Cutoff
WHITE BIRD
John Day Creek
Snake River
RIGGINS
Salmon River
95
NEW MEADOWS
McCALL

Pullouts along the highway offer great vantage points.

White Bird Battlefield was the site of the first major battle of the Nez Perce War. See page 87 for details.

White Bird Summit offers a spectacular view that separates northern Idaho from southern Idaho.

Grangeville, the county seat of Idaho County, offers several good restaurants located along main street, just south of Highway 95.

Cottonwood has all the conveniences of a small town including gas, food, and lodging. Medical facilities are also available.

Getting There

From the northeast end of McCall on Highway 55, head north toward New Meadows. At New Meadows, head north on Highway 95, passing through Riggins, past White Bird, and on to Camas Prairie. At Mile 87, two miles before Grangeville, you can take a paved short cut, Johnston Road, that bypasses Grangeville, and cuts four miles from the trip. If you take the cut-off, you will reconnect with Highway 95 after two miles, where you will turn left (northwest). If you choose not to take the cutoff, stay on Highway 95, and it will take you northeast past Grangeville, before heading west again to Cottonwood. Stay on Highway 95 for approximately sixteen miles until you see the turnoff to Cottonwood. Take the turnoff and go through Cottonwood. At the end of Cottonwood, the road will veer left. Follow the signs three miles to the Monastery of St. Gertrude

Caution

The highway between New Meadows and Riggins in the Little Salmon River Canyon is in a constant state of construction. The road is winding and narrow, with no passing lanes and few turnouts.

Miscellaneous Information

In August of each year, the Monastery of St. Gertrude hosts its Raspberry Festival. The event features live music, classic cars, a quilt show, cultural demonstrations, and great food. Raspberry products are on sale, and all proceeds support the museum. Call for date and time.

History

The Benedictines have a long history in Camas Prairie. In 1903, a group of Benedictine Fathers from Missouri arrived to build St. Michael's Priory, two miles northwest of the present convent. The order was brought to the prairie at the request of several Cottonwood residents, one of whom donated the land.

The nuns, whose order originated in Switzerland, arrived in the United States in 1882 and settled at the monastery in Gervais, Oregon. In 1884, they started a convent, St. Andrews, in Uniontown, Washington, and established schools in various communities in the area. A falling out with the Uniontown priest in 1892 led the nuns to move to Colton, Washington, where they remained for the next several years.

In 1906, after corresponding with several Cottonwood citizens, the nuns sought permission to move to the Camas Prairie. A local resident donated 120 acres to their cause, and they purchased another 370 acres, all of it rich farmland. In December, Pope Pius X gave his permission, and the nuns began arriving the next year.

Work on the chapel and convent began in 1919, with the nuns doing much of the labor. Completed in 1925, the chapel features locally cut stone and an alter imported from Germany. That same year, St. Michael's Priory closed, the priests left Cottonwood, and the sisters took over their property.

With the convent and chapel completed, the nuns turned their attention to their mission of helping others. In 1927, they opened a boarding school and a grade school. While these were eventually closed, the nuns opened St. Gertrude's Academy, a high school, in 1954. Located adjacent to the convent, it operated until 1970. During this time, they also staffed thirteen elementary schools in Idaho and operated several hospitals.

The museum was started in 1931 by Sister M. Alfreda Elsensohn, a historian. Her two volume book, *Pioneer Days in Idaho County*, gives a comprehensive look at the early history of Central Idaho, much of it preserved in the museum. Expanded over the years, the present museum was completed in 1980.

The collection includes Nez Perce artifacts, pioneer exhibits, and military and weaponry displays. In addition, the museum is home to the Rhoades Emmanuel Memorial Exhibit, a fine collection of Asian and European artistry, including some from the Ming Dynasty. Nowhere in Idaho, or in the Pacific Northwest, will you find a more interesting or eclectic collection.

For more information

Museum of St. Gertrude
HC3 Box 121 Keuterville Road
Cottonwood, Idaho 83522
(208) 962-7123
www/webpak.net/~museum

White Bird Battlefield

Description

A scenic, historical drive, this trip takes you to the White Bird Battlefield, site of the first battle of the Nez Perce War. On the way you will pass through the Salmon River Canyon where many of the events that led to the war took place.

Distance/Direction/Road Conditions

The battlefield is situated eighty miles north of McCall with paved highway all the way.

Best Time to Travel

June is the best to make this trip as the weather is mild. If you go in July and August, be prepared for temperatures in the 90s and above. If possible, avoid the weekends when traffic tends to be heavier along the Salmon River.

Facilities

Although facilities are not specifically at the battlefield, picnic sites and camping areas are available along the way. The small community of White Bird also features a general store, two restaurants, a motel, and service station.

Camping

The Slate Creek Recreation area offers picnic tables, restroom facilities, and overnight camping.

Swiftwater RV park and store also has camping sites. It is located on the Salmon River, two miles south of White Bird on old Highway 95.

On the Way

Zim's Hot Springs, four miles north of New Meadows, is open to the public, for a fee. It is a great place for a soak on the return trip home.

Sheep Creek and Slate Creek rest areas–Miles 38 and 68

Riggins–Several good restaurants serve meals all day. For

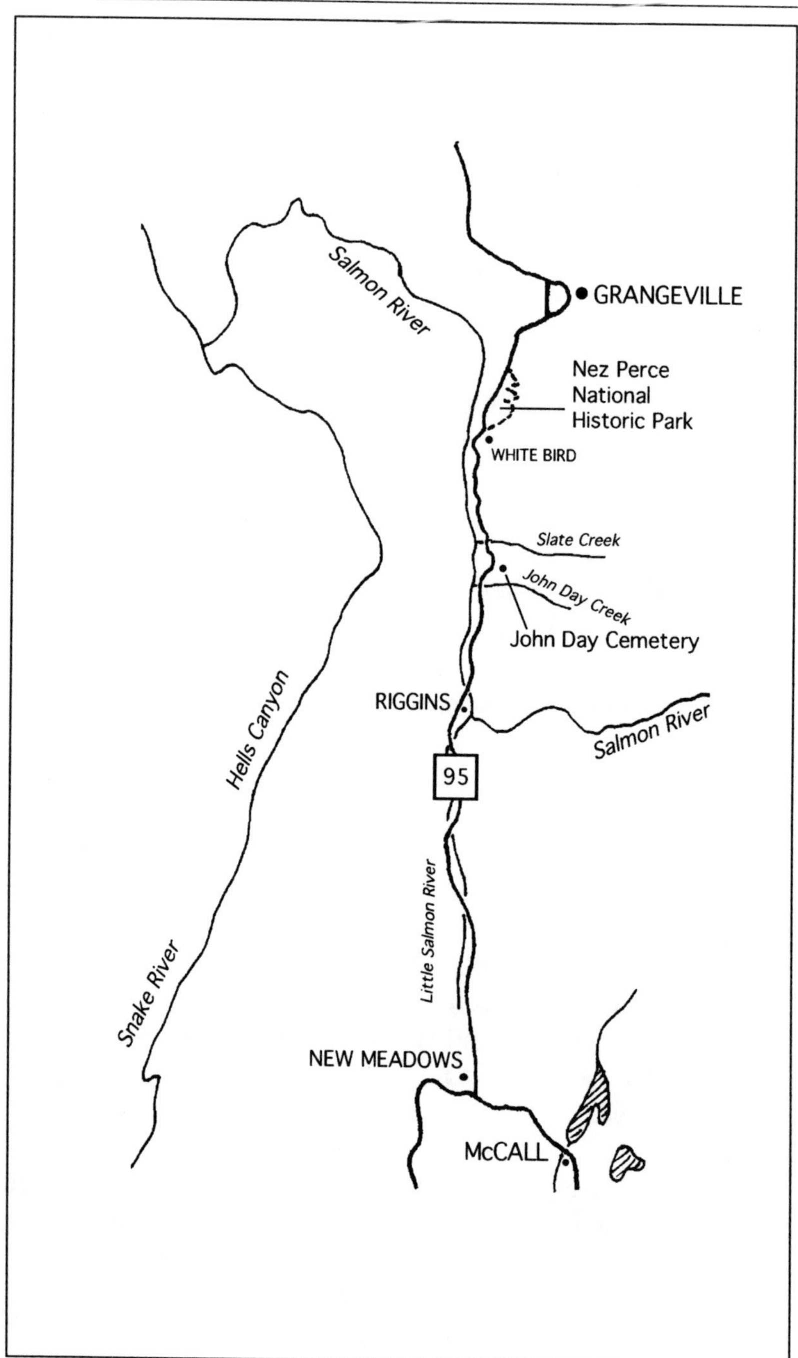
Salmon River
GRANGEVILLE
Nez Perce
National
Historic Park
WHITE BIRD
Slate Creek
John Day Creek
John Day Cemetery
Hells Canyon
RIGGINS
Salmon River
95
Little Salmon River
Snake River
NEW MEADOWS
McCALL

dinner, try the Seven Devils Saloon on Main Street. Two convenience stores offer snacks, cold drinks, and gasoline.

Time Zone Bridge is one mile north of Riggins. On the north side of the bridge, you are in the Pacific Time Zone.

Mining activity–North of the Time Zone Bridge, mining activity, both past and present, is clearly evident on both sides of the river. Watch for mine shafts on the east side of the highway. Just past Lucille, six miles north of Time Zone Bridge, two historical markers give information on Idaho's mining history. One is about Florence, the first mining camp in Central Idaho; the other discusses hydraulic mining techniques used along the Salmon River.

John Day Creek is sixty miles from McCall. One-quarter mile north of the highway, on the knoll overlooking Highway 95 and the Salmon River, is the John Day cemetery. The first white settlers of the Salmon River country are buried here, including the first four victims of what led to the Nez Perce War.

Slate Creek Ranger Station–In the 1870s, this place was called Freedom. Settlers along the river fled to this spot to escape the Indians in the first days of the Nez Perce uprising.

Skookumchuck, at Mile 72.2, is a good picnic spot.

Getting There

From the northeast end of McCall on Highway 55, head north toward New Meadows. At New Meadows, head north on Highway 95; you will pass Riggins, Lucille, and the turnoff to the town of White Bird. Stay on the main highway. As you drive up White Bird Hill, you will see on the right the old highway, your return route. The White Bird Battle historical marker is located at Mile 77 and gives you a great overview of the battle. After stopping at the marker, continue up the hill to Mile 80, to the turnoff to the old highway. This is not marked, but the road takes off to the right. Follow the old highway down the hill. As you near the base of the hill, a monument stands on the east side of the road to commemorate soldiers killed in the White Bird Battle. One-half mile past the monument, the road passes a shale outcropping. This is known as Fossil Rock. Here you can find fossils on almost every piece of rock you examine. Continue toward the community of White Bird, another 1.7 miles. On your right you will find the walking trail that takes you through the White Bird Battlefield. A trail guide is available here and gives you detailed information of the actual battle.

Back on the road, you will make your way into the community of White Bird. Continue on the old road, following White Bird Creek, under the big bridge, to the Salmon River. Approximately two miles from White Bird, on the east side of the old highway, is the French Cemetery, burial site of the white settlers killed by the Indians prior to the White Bird battle. Continue heading south on the old highway, which will take you back to Highway 95.

Caution

Highway 95, from New Meadows to Riggins, is in a constant state of construction. The road is also narrow and winding as it follows the Little Salmon River. Also, be aware of heavy traffic along the Salmon River between Riggins and White Bird, which is very busy on the weekends.

Miscellaneous Information

The White Bird Battlefield is just one site of the Nez Perce National Historic Park, whose headquarters is located at Spalding, Idaho, eleven miles east of Lewiston. The visitors' center at Spalding features displays of the Nez Perce culture and history, plus information on the Nez Perce War. The park features thirty-eight sites, scattered throughout Oregon, Idaho, and Montana. An auto guide to the entire park is available at the headquarters, as is a self-guided walking tour of the White Bird site. These guides are also available at the White Bird site, on occasion.

History

The Nez Perce Indians, the Nee-Me-Poo, originally inhabited the lands of northeast Oregon, southeast Washington and Central Idaho. Organized into bands, with a chief at the head of each, they lived in relative peace with neighboring tribes and covered the areas around the Clearwater, Snake and Salmon

Members of the US Cavalry and a band of volunteers stood on this knoll just prior to the Battle of White Bird.

Rivers. It was the Nez Perce who rescued Lewis and Clark after their wanderings in the Bitterroot Mountains of Montana. While this chance first meeting with white men proved friendly, it was only a matter of time before conflict arose.

Missionary Henry Spaulding arrived in 1836, establishing a mission near Lapwai, Idaho. While he was successful in converting a few of the Nez Perce bands to Christianity, his job was difficult at best. What he managed to do was fracture the Indians, with one group embracing the white man's culture and the other following the traditional ways of the tribe.

In 1847 the massacre at the Whitman Mission in Walla Walla by Cayuse Indians led to the closure of the Spalding Mission; it did not stop the intrusion of whites into Nez Perce land. In 1855, in an attempt to open more land for settlement, the government worked out a treaty with many tribes of the Pacific Northwest, the Nez Perce included. This treaty gave the Nez Perce most of their original homeland, almost seven million acres.

But the influx of white settlers into Indian territory was just beginning. In 1860, gold was discovered in Nez Perce Country, and thousands of prospectors came to the area, all demanding the Indians be removed. In 1863, with the intent of limiting Nez Perce land, the government called for another treaty council. Here, the government proposed limiting the Nez Perce lands to 700,000 acres near Lapwai. When the proposal was made, several of the chiefs of the traditional Nez Perce left the council, angered and insulted by the offer. The remaining chiefs, although not representative of the entire tribe, signed the treaty. The government accepted the treaty and believed all Nez Perce were bound by it. Immediately, white settlers began moving into traditional Nez Perce land.

The few nontreaty bands stayed on their homeland, but complaints against them by the white settlers increased. In the spring of 1877, the government took action to bring all Nez Perce Indians to the reservation at Lapwai. At a council meeting on May 14, 1877, General Oliver Howard gave the nontreaty Indian Chiefs, including Joseph, White Bird, Looking Glass, and Toohoolhoolzote, one month to move their bands to the reservation. The Indians relunctantly complied and on June 13, the nontreaty Indians had made their way to Tolo Lake, near the reservation, six miles west of Grangeville and fifteen miles north of White Bird.

The first settlers arrived in White Bird in the late 1860s, establishing home sites along White Bird Creek and the east side of the Salmon River. A few also settled on the west side of the Main Salmon. Settlers here were gold miners and stock ranchers, several of them with families. Others operated general stores, selling supplies to both settlers and Indians. Indians were often mistreated by the settlers, and this mistreatment led to the uprising.

In 1875, a Nez Perce chief, War Eagle, was killed by a white settler, Larry Ott. Ott, who lived several miles upriver from White Bird, went unpunished for the deed. On the night of June 13, 1877, War Eagle's son, Shore Crossing, was taunted by other

Indians for not avenging his father's death. It was not the time for such teasing. Gathered at Tolo Lake, the Nez Perce were saddened and angry for their forced move to the reservation. They were ready to fight, and they were drinking too much. Shore Crossing reacted by taking two of his friends and riding south to White Bird, then up the Salmon River, in search of Ott. When they did not find him, they headed further upriver, found four other settlers, and killed them.

When word of the murders reached the Indian encampment, it served as a catalyst. The Nez Perce uprising began in earnest. Over the next two days, nine more settlers in and around White Bird were killed by the Nez Perce. At the same time, settlers on the Camas Prairie were attacked and killed. When word of the uprising reached Fort Lapwai, government troops were sent to put down the insurrection.

Companies F and H of the 1st US Cavalry left Lapwai on the afternoon of June 15. Under the direction of Captain David Perry, they were 103 strong. They rode all night and day, and in the evening of June 16, they reached Grangeville. Here they were joined by eleven volunteers. In the dark of night, they headed south, stopping to camp at the head of White Bird Canyon. Early the next morning, they continued down the canyon in search of the Nez Perce.

The Nez Perce were camped on White Bird Creek, on the floor of the canyon, when they learned of the approaching troops. After much discussion, they decided to send a truce party to meet the cavalry, while at the same time, they prepared for battle.

As the detachment from the cavalry descended deeper into the canyon, federal scouts reported they were approaching the Indian encampment. One of the volunteers broke away from the group to see for himself. What he saw was the truce party. The volunteer fired, and the Battle of White Bird began. When it was over, thirty-four soldiers were dead. The Nez Perce suffered no casualties.

The White Bird battle marked the beginning of the Nez Perce

historic flight for freedom. The Indians, led by Chief Joseph, evaded capture for three months before surrendering to Federal troops in Montana in October, 1877.

For More Information

Nez Perce National Historical Park
Route 1, Box 100
Highway 95
Spalding, Idaho 83540
(208) 843-2261

For Future Reading

Following the Nez Perce Trail
by Cheryl Wilfong

Forlorn Hope
by John McDermott

Roseberry

Description

At one time the biggest town in Valley County, Roseberry virtually disappeared when the railroad came through. Today its museum and other exhibits show visitors what Valley County was like in the early 1900s.

Distance/Direction/Road Conditions

Roseberry is located thirteen miles south of McCall, with pavement all the way.

Best Time to Travel

Any day of the week is a great time to travel to Roseberry, although the museum is only open Friday through Sunday. The drive itself is best in the morning or early evening.

Facilities

Roseberry is home to the Valley County Museum, open Friday through Sunday, 1-5 p.m. The Roseberry General Store is also open and worth a visit. Besides cold drinks, ice cream, and snacks, the store is filled with artifacts of Valley County's early Finnish culture.

Camping

None is available, although there are picnic tables at the site.

On the Way

Elo School, Finn Church, and Spink Cemetery are all part of Valley County's rich Finnish heritage (see Farm to Market, page 31.)

Caution

People have a tendency to drive too fast on this country road. This is also open range land. Keep an eye out for cattle and deer.

Getting There

From the south end of McCall, head south on Highway 55. Turn left (east) on Elo Road, one mile from McCall. This road

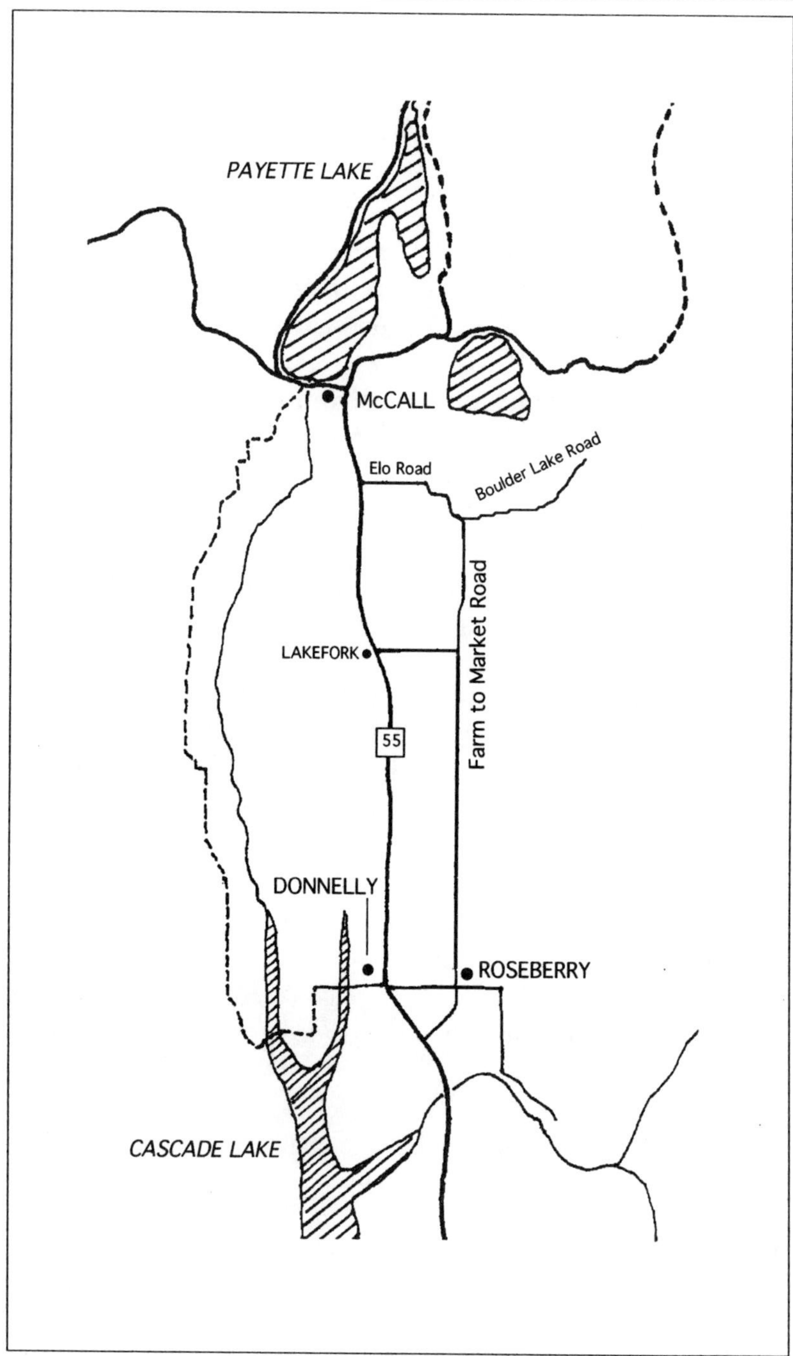
PAYETTE LAKE
McCALL
Elo Road
Boulder Lake Road
Farm to Market Road
LAKEFORK
55
DONNELLY
ROSEBERRY
CASCADE LAKE

The general store at Roseberry

will make several sharp turns for the next few miles. After three miles on Elo Road, the road will fork. Take the fork to the right (south), and you are on Farm to Market Road. Follow this road straight to Roseberry. To return home, take the same route, or head west to Donnelly on East Roseberry Road. From there, Highway 55 will take you the eleven miles back to McCall.

History

Roseberry prospered less than twenty years before giving way to progress and the railroad.

Roseberry was founded in 1891 by Lewis Roseberry; the Roseberry home became the first post office. Soon after, H.T. Boydstun established a general store and families began settling in the area. By 1907, the town was booming and the leaders of Roseberry decided to incorporate, selling lots and promoting the community to outsiders. The Commercial Club of Roseberry led the advance, putting the town in the best light. The club produced a booklet "Long Valley as Seen Through the Camera," and explained that city lots would not be sold to vendors of intoxicating drinks or indecent resorts. This would ensure that the right class of people would settle Roseberry.

Whether by design or chance, Roseberry did grow. By 1910, some accounts estimate its population at 1,000. The town featured a bank, a general store, a hardware store, a twenty-three bed hotel, a saw mill, a flour mill, and a creamery. It also had its own newspaper, *The Long Valley Advocate*, and provided schooling for students with an elementary and a high school.

In keeping with its clean image, Roseberry also had two churches. The first, intended to be a community church, was built in 1904 by local residents with the financial help of the Methodist/Episcopal Diocese. The Diocese paid for the doors and windows and then demanded its name on the church. Offended residents responded by building a new church, this one known as the Community Christian Church.

But even two churches and solid growth could not save Roseberry from the railroad. While Roseberry's leaders made offers to get the rail line into the community, the Short Line Railroad chose to locate 1.5 miles to the west, and the town of Donnelly was created. When the rail line reached Long Valley in 1913, it was clear Roseberry's prosperity was over.

Not to miss out, many of Roseberry's businessmen picked up their establishments and, literally, moved to Donnelly. Over the next few years several buildings from Roseberry, including the bank, the livery stable, and both churches, were dragged across the valley floor by teams of horses and reestablished in Donnelly.

Slowly, Roseberry went the way of all boom towns. The high school closed in 1928, the last business, the McDougal store, in 1939. Finally, in 1942, the post office locked its doors, and Roseberry officially became a memory.

In recent years that memory has been revived, thanks to the efforts of the Long Valley Preservation Society. Formed in 1972, the group has worked tirelessly to restore Roseberry and preserve the history of Long Valley. In 1973, the Methodist church was moved back to Roseberry to its original spot. The building now houses the Valley County Museum. Other historic buildings have been moved to the site and will eventually become a part of Roseberry's restoration.

To celebrate Roseberry, the Society sponsors an ice cream social every Labor Day. The event is open to the public and serves as a fund raiser for restoration projects.

Other events hosted in Roseberry include the McCall Arts and Crafts Fair, on the first weekend in July and the McCall Music Festival, held the third weekend in July.

Another sign of revival in Roseberry is the Roseberry General Store which reopened in 2003. The store serves as a gathering point for locals and tourists alike. Make sure to check out its historical products and displays.

For More Information

Valley County Museum
13131 Farm to Market Road
Donnelly, Idaho 83615
(208) 325-8628

Big Creek

Description

The gateway to Idaho's Frank Church River of No Return Wilderness, Big Creek is a peaceful, scenic back-country getaway.

Distance/Direction/Road Conditions

Big Creek is located seventy-four miles east of McCall. The route leaves McCall's east side and travels over Lick Creek Summit, past Yellow Pine, over Profile Summit, and into the Big Creek Valley. The Forest Service maintains the well-traveled, gravel road, which can be extremely rough at times. It is not recommended for RVs or vehicles pulling trailers.

Best Time to Travel

The road is usually open late June to mid-October, depending on snowfall. Contact the Payette National Forest for current road conditions. If you want the road to yourself, weekdays are the best time to travel.

Facilities

At one time, guests had their choice of two lodges in Big Creek where visitors could get a meal and spend the night. At the present time only one lodge, Big Creek Lodge, is open to the public. Always call ahead to make sure the lodge is open. No other facilities are available.

Camping

On the way, two Forest Service campgrounds make great rest stops. Ponderosa Campground, at Mile 30, sits on the banks of the Secesh River and the start of the Secesh River Trail. Yellow Pine Campground, a half-mile south of Yellow Pine on the Johnson Creek Road, is a good place to rest before you start the last leg to Big Creek. Both campgrounds feature water, picnic tables, fire rings, and pit toilets.

In Big Creek, a Forest Service campground with picnic tables,

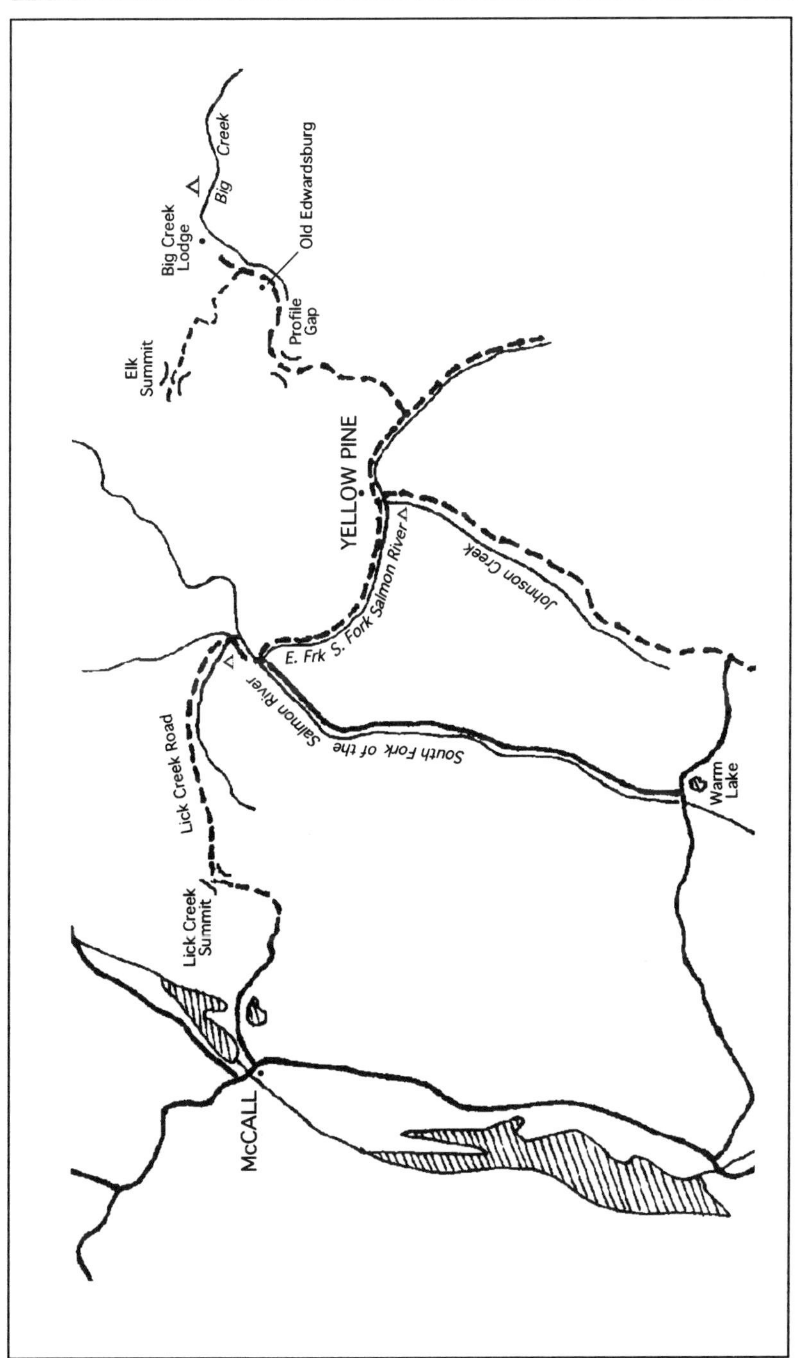
Big Creek
Big Creek Lodge
Old Edwardsburg
Profile Gap
Elk Summit
YELLOW PINE
E. Frk S. Fork Salmon River
Johnson Creek
South Fork of the Salmon River
Lick Creek Road
Lick Creek Summit
Warm Lake
McCALL

fire rings, and pit toilets is available. It is located at the south end of the Big Creek airstrip and is the starting point for hikers heading into the wilderness area.

On the Way

Little Lake at Mile 5 offers trout and bass fishing.

Brown's Pond, a popular fishing spot, is located eight miles into the drive. Huckleberries are also plentiful on the west end of the pond and are usually ready to pick in mid-July.

Lakefork Campground–Forest Service site with picnic tables and pit toilets

Lick Creek Summit–elevation 6,879 feet

Duck Lake Trail Head–At Mile 20, an easy trail leads to Duck Lake, a small but pretty high-mountain lake. The trail is suitable for young children.

Zena Creek–A logging camp in the 1950s, Zena Creek also served as an outfitter's lodge. Cabins are available to rent at the site.

Chinese Rock House–Found at Mile 35 on the east side of the road across the river, the rock house is clearly visible. A Forest Service interpretive sign explains the house and the presence of Chinese miners in the area.

Yellow Pine–see page 43.

Profile Summit is at elevation 7,605 feet. Profile Sam Willson had several mines in the area. A monument to him is located on the west side of the road.

Gillihan's Lodge at Mile 73 is the original site of Edwardsburg, first settlement in Big Creek.

Caution

Lick Creek Road and the road over Profile Summit are steep and rugged. While they are regularly maintained, heavy traffic and sudden rainstorms can cause havoc. In some places, they are just one lane roads, so be ready to use the turnouts. Drive with caution. Also be aware of wildlife, especially deer, on the roadway.

Getting There

From the east side of McCall, past the McCall Golf Course,

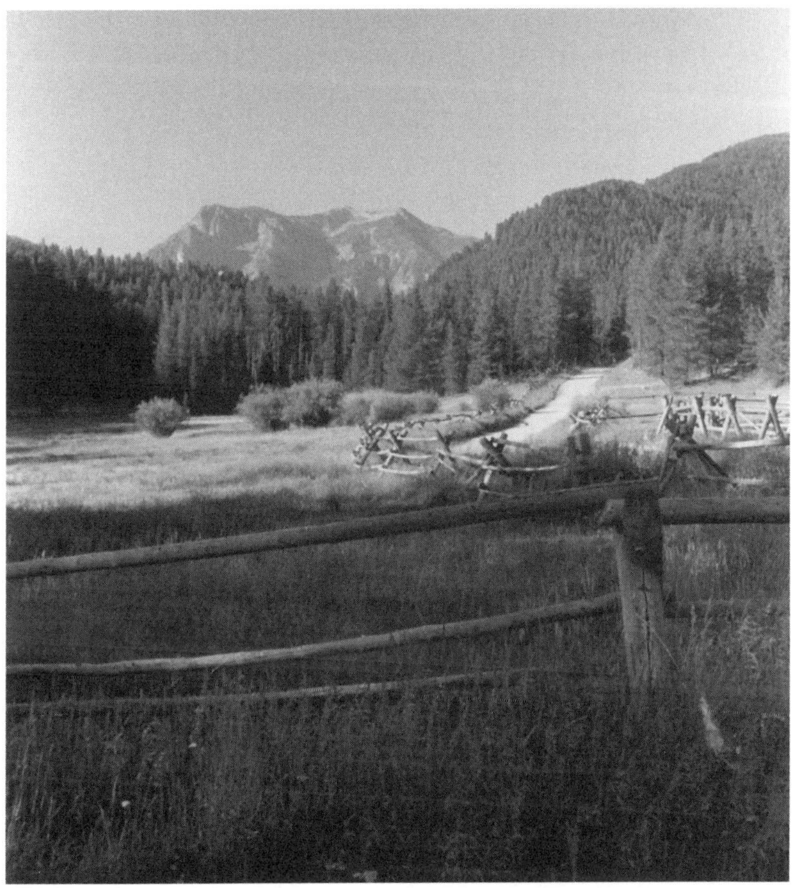

The meadow across from Big Creek Lodge

head east on Lick Creek Road. After two miles, the road will split; you continue straight on Lick Creek Road. The road to the left becomes East Side Drive. Follow Lick Creek Road forty-five miles. Here you will come to the junction of Lick Creek Road, Yellow Pine, and Johnson Creek Road. Continue straight on Lick Creek Road. You will be following the East Fork of the South Fork of the Salmon River. At Mile 55.2 the road will fork. Turn left here on FS Road 340. You will now be heading north. This road will take you over Profile Summit before dropping down into Big Creek. At Mile 73.4, you will reach the summer home area of Big Creek. Continue past these homes. FS340 will take off to your left. You continue straight, one more mile to the Big Creek Lodge, airstrip, and campground.

Miscellaneous Information

The wild flowers on this route are remarkable, especially in mid-July. There is also excellent fishing as you follow the East Fork of the South Fork of the Salmon River. Make sure you check fishing regulations for the area if you decide to try your luck. Finally, if you take this trip in late July or early August, you must stop along Big Creek and watch for the salmon which are usually spawning during this time. It is a sight you will not forget.

History

Unlike most of the abandoned mining towns around McCall, Big Creek was never a boom town, in spite of the best intentions. It was home to many trappers and miners and transients over the years, but the isolated location and the ore which would not give up its gold discouraged even the most diligent of miners.

With the discovery of gold in Warren in 1862, thousands of miners moved into the area. The search for gold led miners to the South Fork of the Salmon and then over the mountains into the Big Creek drainage. Many of these miners landed on Logan Creek, which cuts through the summer home area of the Big Creek community. A one lane mountain road follows Logan Creek to the remains of the Sunday, Ludwig, and Moscow mines.

In the late 1800s, the Caswell brothers found gold on what is now called Mule Creek, and the Thunder Mountain gold rush was on. Miners made their way to Thunder Mountain following the Three Blaze Trail. Constructed in 1901, it led from the gold fields in Dixie, across the Salmon River to Thunder Mountain, and brought an influx of miners to the Big Creek area.

In 1902, William Edwards, a southern lawyer with knowledge of mining law, set out for Idaho. He had researched the Thunder Mountain area before arriving and eventually concluded there was more talk than gold in the hills there. How-

Part of the Big Creek Lodge

ever, he was intrigued by the Big Creek country. He was truly convinced a vast mineral belt lay on Logan Creek. In 1903 he purchased several claims there, and in 1904 moved to the area for good with his wife and young son, arriving by trail from Warren over Elk Summit.

Edwards built a large log house and worked his mining claims, among them Copper Camp, located on Camp Creek, east of the Big Creek airstrip. His wife, Annie, ran the post office, originally called the Logan Post Office, out of their home. In 1909, he established the town of Edwardsburg and changed the name of the post office. He used his powers of persuasion to earn the trust and bankrolls of some wealthy friends who invested heavily in his Sunday Mine. Unfortunately for Edwards and the investors, the mine failed.

However, Edwards was savvy enough to file a homestead claim on 160 acres of his Big Creek land, and he was granted a patent in 1924. Shortly after, his son Annesley Napier Edwards filed a homestead claim for land adjacent to his father's. This patent, for 152 acres, was granted in 1928.

Between 1920 and 1940, Edwardsburg attracted individual miners and the Forest Service. Mining companies leased claims in the area for exploration, but none made the committment to operate in the isolated area. In 1922, to bridge the isolation, improvements began on the wagon road from Warren, making it suitable for automobile traffic. This project was completed in 1924. Shortly after, the Forest Service constructed its first headquarters in Big Creek along with a commissary and storage area.

Transportation to Edwardsburg was further improved in the 1930s as the Civilian Conservation Corps built a road from Yellow Pine to Edwardsburg. This allowed miners and visitors to reach the area via Cascade and Yellow Pine. This eventually became the preferred route into the Big Creek area. Soon after, a hotel opened at the site of the present day Big Creek Lodge providing rooms and meals. A gas station, store, and the Big Creek Post Office were also located there.

Even with improved transportation and better roads, Big Creek failed to thrive as its gold remained elusive. Edwards's attempts to establish lucrative mines fell short; gold found in the area had to be crushed or leached, processes that were both dangerous and expensive. Complicating the problem was World War II; the government placed a moratorium on gold mining, and the mines of Edwardsburg went silent. By the time the moratorium was lifted, long winters and heavy snows had rusted equipment and caved in mines. Gold was selling for only $18 an ounce, hardly worth the cost of rebuilding the mines or repairing the equipment.

After the war, government regulations concerning mining added to the problems. Miners were not allowed to build cabins on their claims, and tent living in Big Creek was marginal at best. When assessment costs went from $100 to $200 a year, many miners gave up their claims and the government took over.

Still, some remained and continued to work their claims. Others turned to trapping, packing, logging, and freighting. Some became farmers and raised cattle and produce which they sold to the mines still in operation. Big mining companies sent teams of geologists and surveyors to study the area for future mining development. The Big Creek Lodge and Gillihan's Lodge, located at the original site of William Edwards's homestead, provided back-country hospitality to these visitors who in turn sustained their businesses. Travelers to central Idaho could take the two-day South Fork loop traveling from McCall to Warren to Big Creek to Yellow Pine and then back to McCall, stopping in Big Creek for the night. Hunters flocked to the area in the fall, and outfitters, many of them originally miners, led parties on successful elk hunts. Idaho Fish and Game, to accommodate the hunters, kept the road to Big Creek open through December.

By the late 1990s, however, interest in the Big Creek area declined. While some mining companies and a handful of miners still have interests in the area, government restrictions, transportation problems, and lack of power make a modern mining operation impractical. In 1993, the road from the South Fork over Elk Summit to Big Creek washed out. While a rebuilding project began in 2000, the road has yet to reopen, and no completion date for the project has been announced. Because hunting seasons in and around Big Creek have been shortened, Fish and Game no longer plows the road from Yellow Pine. As a result, access to the area by vehicle is limited to just five months of the year. Gillihan's no longer books overnight guests, although Snow Bank Outfitters still operates out of the lodge. Changes may also be in store for the Big Creek Lodge as the lodge is presently for sale.

What the future holds for Big Creek is unclear. A few miners still work their claims in the area, and some of the residences have become well-maintained summer homes. The Forest Service continues to have a presence. Snowmobiles have opened up the area, allowing the adventurous to enjoy the back-country even in the heart of winter. One thing for sure is clear: Big Creek is a beautiful spot in the heart of Idaho.

For More Information

Payette National Forest
Krassel Ranger District
P.O. Box 1026
500 N. Mission
McCall, Idaho 83638
(208) 634-0600

Big Creek Lodge
Big Creek, Idaho
(888) 848-0011
Radio Call: (208) 382-4336 and ask for Big Creek

Pittsburg Landing

Description

The drive to Pittsburg Landing, over Pittsburg Saddle, is most memorable. From the saddle the view of the Snake and Salmon River Canyons is breathtaking.

Distance/Direction/Conditions

Pittsburg Landing is located ninety miles northwest of McCall. The first seventy-three miles of the route are paved, after which it becomes an improved dirt road. The dirt road is steep and narrow in spots, but well maintained with frequent pull-outs.

Best time to Travel

May, early-June, September, and October are the prime times to take this drive. While the road is kept open in the winter, rain and snow make the drive miserable. Temperatures in July and August frequently hit triple digits and very little shade is available.

Facilities

Only restrooms are available at the landing. Restaurants, convenience stores, and gas stations can be found on the way, in Riggins.

Camping

Hammer Creek Campground, on the Salmon River, is one mile downriver from the turnoff to Pittsburg Landing. A hot, dry campground, it features water and pit toilets. It is the launching point for raft trips traveling the lower Salmon River.

Pittsburg Landing Campground accommodates both tents and RV camping at the lower landing. Water and pit toilets are available. At the upper landing, only tent camping is allowed.

On the Way

Sheep Creek Rest Area at Mile 38, a well-maintained rest area, features restroom facilities and a picnic area.

Riggins–Several good restaurants serve meals throughout the day. The community also has two well-stocked convenience stores

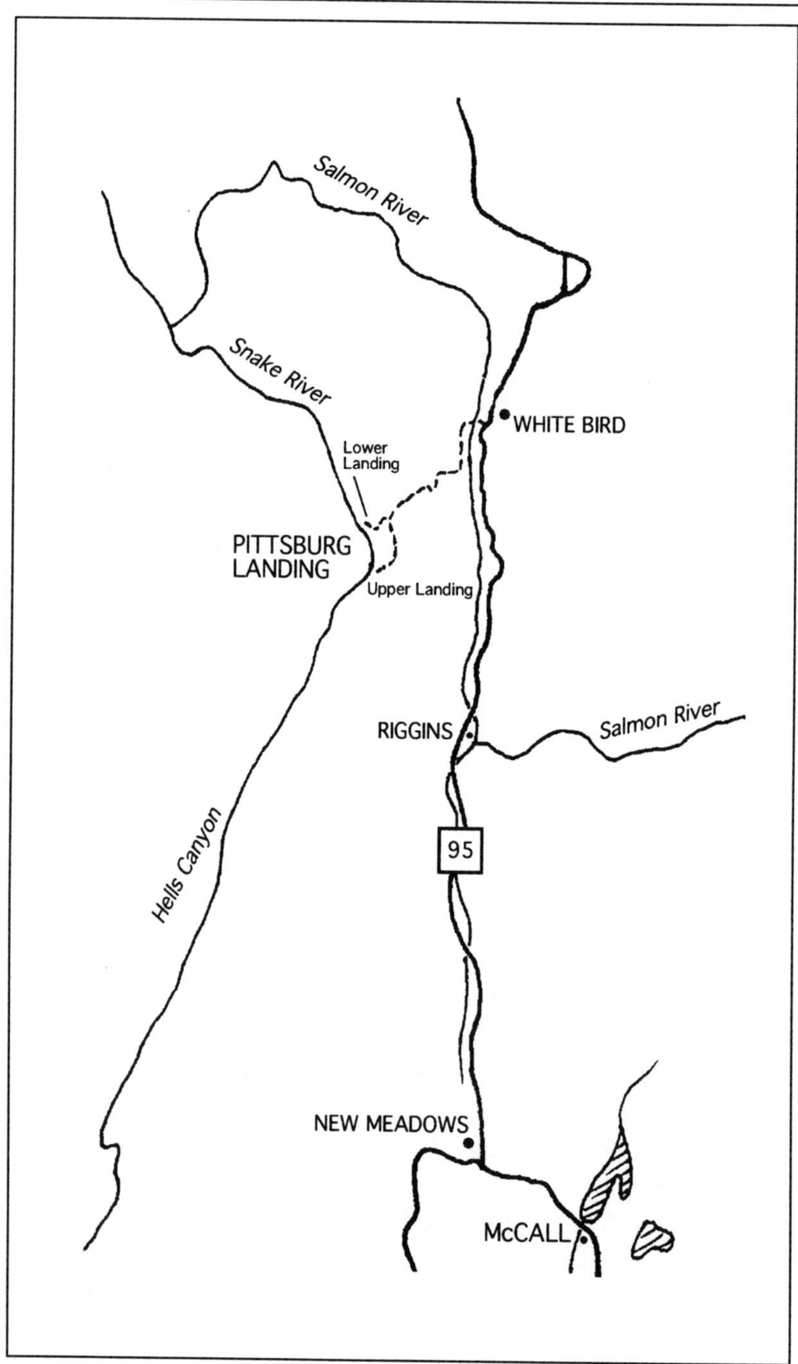
Salmon River
Snake River
WHITE BIRD
Lower Landing
PITTSBURG LANDING
Upper Landing
RIGGINS
Salmon River
95
Hells Canyon
NEW MEADOWS
McCALL

and several gas stations.

Slate Creek Rest and Camping area at Mile 64 is the last rest area before heading to the Snake River. It features restrooms, picnic tables, and access to the Salmon River.

Pittsburg Saddle–This is a great place to stop to get a scenic view of the Snake River Canyon. A picnic table and interpretive information are located here.

Caution

Highway 95 between McCall and Riggins can be very busy during the summer. It is also in a constant state of construction, so be ready for delays. The dirt road to the landing can be a dusty washboard at times, and as any mountain road, it is narrow in spots with some blind curves. Be prepared for traffic pulling jet boats and rafts. Also on the road, deer are plentiful on both sides of the saddle, so keep your eyes peeled. Finally, the Snake River Canyon is not kind to hikers who aren't mindful of the dangers of poison ivy and rattlesnakes. Be alert if you decide to explore the areas around the landing.

Getting There

From McCall, head northeast on Highway 55 to New Meadows. Turn north on to Highway 95 and follow it through Riggins and along the Salmon River. At Mile 71.8, signs will direct you to turn left off the highway toward Pittsburg Landing. This is a blind corner, so use caution. Follow this road for one mile. You will come to a bridge crossing the Salmon River. Turn left at the bridge. Immediately following the bridge, turn left again. Follow this main road for the next seventeen miles to the landing. At Mile 89.5, a road will take off to the left and lead to the upper landing and the Indian artifacts. If you go straight, it will take you directly to the lower landing.

Miscellaneous Information

Pittsburg Landing is not the best destination; it can be a long dusty drive, and summer heat can make it unbearable. But a springtime drive to the Landing is definitely worthwhile. You will not be disappointed by the canyon scenery, the colorful wild flowers, or the abundant wildlife.

Petroglyphs at Pittsburg Landing

History

Pittsburg Landing was occupied by the Nez Perce Indians long before any white men traveled through the area. Archeological evidence of their habitation can be found throughout the area. Between 1840 and 1870, the landing was used as a winter camp by the Nez Perce Chief Toohoolootze and his band. These Indians were involved in the Battle of White Bird (see page 87).

Visitors can get a glimpse of Indian culture at the upper landing, where a trail and interpretive signs lead to Indian petroglyphs and a large grinding stone. Over the years, the petroglyphs have been vandalized, so the collection is not as impressive as it once was. The grinding stone, however, remains to remind us of the Native American presence in the area.

White men were at the landing as early as 1862, when a group of miners/explorers left Lewiston to investigate the Snake and Salmon Rivers. Conflicting stories explain the name "Pittsburg." Some say the landing was so named because of coal found on a nearby creek; thus, it was named after the coal-town, Pittsburgh, Pennsylvania, and early maps show it listed with the Pittsburg*h* spelling. Others, however, have claimed it was named after Pittsburg Landing, Tennessee, sight of the Battle of Shilo in 1862. This is also the accepted spelling.

The first recorded non-Indian occupancy at the Landing occurred in 1877 on the Idaho side of the Snake River. Henry Kurry settled the upper flat at the landing with his wife and three boys. They homesteaded the property and built their houses out of the flat field stone from the area. They are responsible for the row of osage orange trees located on the north side of the road (Mile 88). The family left its name on the flat as the road to the landing crosses Kurry Creek. Henry Kurry, who died in the 1940s, is buried on the upper flat in an unmarked grave.

The Oregon side of the river was first settled in 1885 by Mike Thomason. Thomason established a large cattle operation and received a homestead patent on the place. He was also the first to operate a ferry at Pittsburg Landing, which began operation in 1891.

In the late 1890s and early 1900s, the landing was well occupied. In 1900, a wagon road over the saddle to the landing was completed, and the following year it was designated a county road. A post office operated between 1905 and 1907, and again from 1910 and 1913. Between 1904 and 1915, twenty-one homestead applications were filed in the area. Of those, eight were granted.

The lower flat and landing area were settled in 1894 by George Wood. He and his family ditched the entire bar to support a two acre garden and 100 acres of hay. They also planted over 100 fruit trees.

In the early 1930s, sixty-one people lived in and around the landing. At that time, the Campbell brothers of Meadows Valley purchased the entire area, making it part of the Circle C Ranch. The ferry closed in October 1933 due to a lack of funds and use. The landing and surrounding area presently is controlled by the Forest Service as part of the Hells Canyon National Recreation Area.

Pittsburg Landing is now a primary put-in and take-out point for boaters on the Snake River. An information and interpretive center is located at the lower landing. The Nez Perce Tribe also manages a Chinook salmon recovery operation at the lower landing. Between March and May of each year, the tribe acclimates 500,000 Chinook salmon to the Snake River, releasing them into the river at the end of May.

For More Information

Hells Canyon National Recreation Area
Highway 95
P.O. Box 832
Riggins, Idaho 83549
(208) 628-3916

Stibnite

Description

In the early 1940s, Stibnite was a boom town, the biggest producer of tungsten and antimony in the United States. While nothing is left of the community, the glory hole remains and is worth the drive for mining and history buffs.

Distance/Direction/Conditions

This route to Stibnite takes you over Warm Lake Summit and down Johnson Creek with a return trip over Lick Creek Summit, a 166 mile trip. The road features sixty-one miles of pavement with the rest improved dirt road. The road following Johnson Creek is in especially good condition and suitable for all vehicles. However, a ten-mile stretch on the east side of Lick Creek Summit is narrow and rough and requires extreme caution.

Best Time to Travel

Weekdays from mid-June to late October, depending on snowfall, are the best time to travel to Stibnite. Fall colors are especially beautiful. Check with the Payette National Forest for road conditions.

Facilities

No facilities are available at Stibnite.

Camping

The Forest Service maintains several campgrounds along the way. All feature water, picnic tables, fire rings, and pit toilets.

South Fork Campground, at Mile 49, sits along the bank of the South Fork of the Salmon River

Buck Mountain Campground–Mile 63

Ice Hole Campground is located at Mile 80. In the early days of Yellowpine, residents of the area obtained their ice at this spot.

Golden Gate Campground–Mile 83

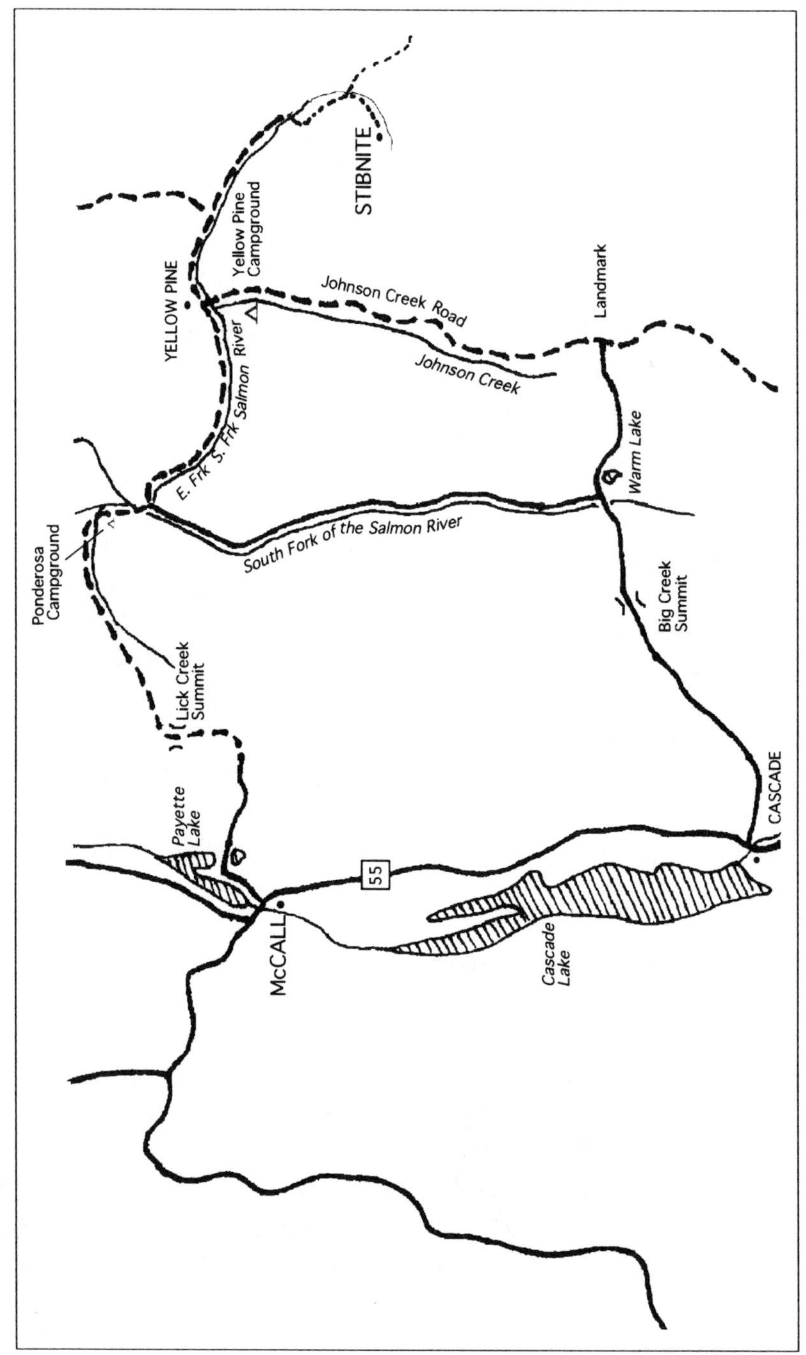
STIBNITE
YELLOW PINE
Yellow Pine Campground
Johnson Creek Road
Johnson Creek
Landmark
E. Frk S. Frk Salmon River
Warm Lake
South Fork of the Salmon River
Ponderosa Campground
Big Creek Summit
Lick Creek Summit
CASCADE
Payette Lake
55
McCALL
Cascade Lake

Yellow Pine Campground–Mile 85

On the Way

Big Creek Summit–elevation 6,549 feet

Warm Lake–Two lodges at Warm Lake, the Warm Lake Lodge and the North Shore Lodge, offer full service dining rooms and may be good stops for an early breakfast.

Warm Lake Summit–elevation 7,291 feet

Wapiti Meadow Ranch–On the Johnson Creek Road, this private wilderness ranch features fishing and hunting excursions, hiking, and horseback riding.

Yellow Pine–A back-country community, Yellow Pine has a general store, a restaurant and bar, and a hotel. It is a great place to stop for a cold drink or ice cream.

Caution

This is big game area, and elk and deer are plentiful around Warm Lake and on the Johnson Creek Road. Traffic can also be heavy on the weekends, especially in and around Warm Lake, so drive defensively.

Getting There

From the south end of McCall, head south on Highway 55. At Mile 26.5, just before you enter Cascade, the Warm Lake Highway will take off to your left. Take this road and travel over Big Creek summit to Warm Lake. Continue past Warm Lake. The road will begin its ascent over Warm Lake Summit and then drop quickly toward Landmark.

At Mile 60.7, you will come to Forest Service Road 413, which leads to Yellow Pine. Turn left on this road and follow it to Yellow Pine. At Mile 85.7, you will reach the junction of Johnson Creek Road and Lick Creek Road. Straight ahead will be Yellow Pine. You will turn right to Stibnite. You will follow this road along the East Fork of the South Fork of the Salmon River for five miles.

At Mile 90.5, the road will fork; the left fork leads to Big Creek while the right fork, FS Road 412, will take you to Stibnite. At Mile 96.5, you will cross Sugar Creek. Continue on FS Road 412, up the hill. At Mile 97.7, you will see the massive Glory

Hole and the remains of old Stibnite.

To return home, retrace your route to the Yellow Pine intersection. Continue heading west on Lick Creek Road. It will return you to McCall.

Miscellaneous

Stibnite endured cycles of prosperity and decline for almost 100 years. In 1999, a massive cleanup began to restore the area. A joint effort by the state and the federal government reclaimed many of the old mining roads, rebuilt several stream channels, refilled some of the excavation pits, and razed most of the buildings. While evidence of mining is still visible, much of what was Stibnite is gone.

History

Gold fever swept through central Idaho mountains in the early 1900s with the Thunder Mountain strike, and miners of all persuasions sought the elusive mineral. While Stibnite never produced the quantity of gold its investors had hoped for, the area did provide a valuable service to America's war effort in the 1940s.

Al Hennessey recorded the first claims in Stibnite, perhaps as early as 1902. Five claims in all, he called them the Meadow Creek claims, and they were located on the southern end of the area now referred to as Stibnite. He worked the claims taking gold, cinnabar, and antimony from underground tunnels.

Hennessey sold the claims to the United Mercury Mines in 1921. He returned to file more claims in 1923 and formed his own mining company, Great Northern Mines. Eventually, United Mercury and Great Northern sold out to the Bradley Mining Company. Bradley took over the entire area, expanded the mining operations, and turned Stibnite into a company town. It was Bradley who expanded the underground operations and created the large open pit mine still visible at Stibnite today.

The company built a road to Yellow Pine, constructed a boarding house and bunk house for workers, and employed a camp cook. A post office was established in 1930. Eventually 100 to 150 people lived and worked in the Stibnite camp, including fifteen families with children.

The Bradley operation struggled for years. The isolated location of the mine, the lack of gold, and the presence of minerals no one wanted, all made for a nonprofitable venture. Then in 1939, the U.S. Bureau of Mines began drilling for antimony. In 1940-41, the drills hit high grade tungsten with antimony, and a new mining boom was on.

With the start of World War II, drilling and digging began in earnest at Stibnite, with miles of tunnels and shafts drilled in the area. Between 1942 and 1945, Stibnite produced fifty percent of the tungsten and ninety-eight percent of the antimony used in the United States. The materials were used in the war effort on such things as aircraft carrier decks and armor piercing shells.

With the renewed interest, Stibnite grew, peaking at a population of 1,500. To accommodate its workers, the Bradley Company built over 100 homes. Every truck that arrived in Stibnite brought supplies and left loaded with ore. Eventually, Stibnite featured a service station, a general store, and a hospital, equipped with a full time doctor, private rooms, and surgical facilities.

The pride of Stibnite, though, was its recreation hall. The two story building featured a movie theater, dance hall, bowling alley, gymnasium, cafe, and library. As with most company towns, though, Stibnite was dry. Miners dying for a drink were forced to drive the treacherous road to Yellow Pine, eighteen miles away. The result was numerous accidents on the return trip home. To solve the problem, the Bradley Company established a club for those inclined to have a drink or two.

While taking care of the adults, the company also looked after the children, building a four-room elementary school. Between 1942 to 1946, it was the largest school in Valley County. From 1943 to 1946, Stibnite also had a high school, with classes held in the recreation hall. For physical education in the winter, the students went cross-country skiing.

Transportation to Stibnite continued to be a problem. Cascade, eighty-three miles away, was the closest rail line and thus the staging point for all materials in and out of Stibnite. The main road ran from Cascade to Warm Lake and Landmark, then down Johnson Creek to Yellow Pine. It was grueling any time of the year, especially in winter. The road was divided into sections, with crews stationed at each section to keep the road open, no matter how deep the snow became. Costs were picked up by the federal government, which also provided snow removal equipment. Between 1942 to 1952, the road remained open all year and during that time, while there were plenty of accidents, no lives were ever lost.

When the war ended, government interest in the mine waned, but the Bradley Company expanded, with an emphasis on gold and gold-antimony ore. The company opened an electric smelter and increased processing to 2,400 tons of ore per day. But the glory days of Stibnite were over. Constant problems with the smelter and a declining economy gave Bradley no choice; it closed the mine in 1952.

What happened next can only be described as back-country ingenuity. When the mine closed, the entire town of Stibnite was virtually abandoned, including 128 houses, all in relatively good condition. While much of the mining equipment was dismantled, the houses were sold intact. They changed hands twice before becoming the property of Warren Campbell of McCall in the late 1950s.

Campbell's plan was simple. Find a buyer for each house, jack it off its foundation, and haul it to wherever the buyer wanted, all for $3,500. For six years, Campbell, with a five-man crew, a pilot car, and a modified logging truck, hauled the 24' x 40' houses from Stibnite to McCall, sixty-five miles on one of the narrowest, roughest roads in the area. To complicate matters, he had to make the trip from Yellow Pine to McCall at night to avoid the numerous logging trucks which used the road during the day.

At first the trip took him seven hours, but as he became more adept at the process, he could transport one of the houses to

McCall in four hours. He moved all 128 houses, losing only one, which slid off the side of the truck as it neared Yellow Pine. The Stibnite houses traveled to as far away as Cambridge, Council, Emmett, Caldwell, and Bruneau, as well as Cascade, New Meadows, Donnelly and McCall. Many of the houses on Davis Street and Hewitt Street (near the McCall Memorial Hospital) were originally Stibnite homes.

With the mine and equipment dismantled, Stibnite went the way of many old mining towns, filled with ghosts and spent dreams. Over the last forty years, efforts have been made to revive the mine, but all have failed. With the reclamation efforts ongoing today, it is likely Stibnite's gold and much of its history will be remain one of Idaho's buried treasures.

For More Information

Payette National Forest
Krassel Ranger District
500 N. Mission
McCall, Idaho 83638
(208) 634-0600

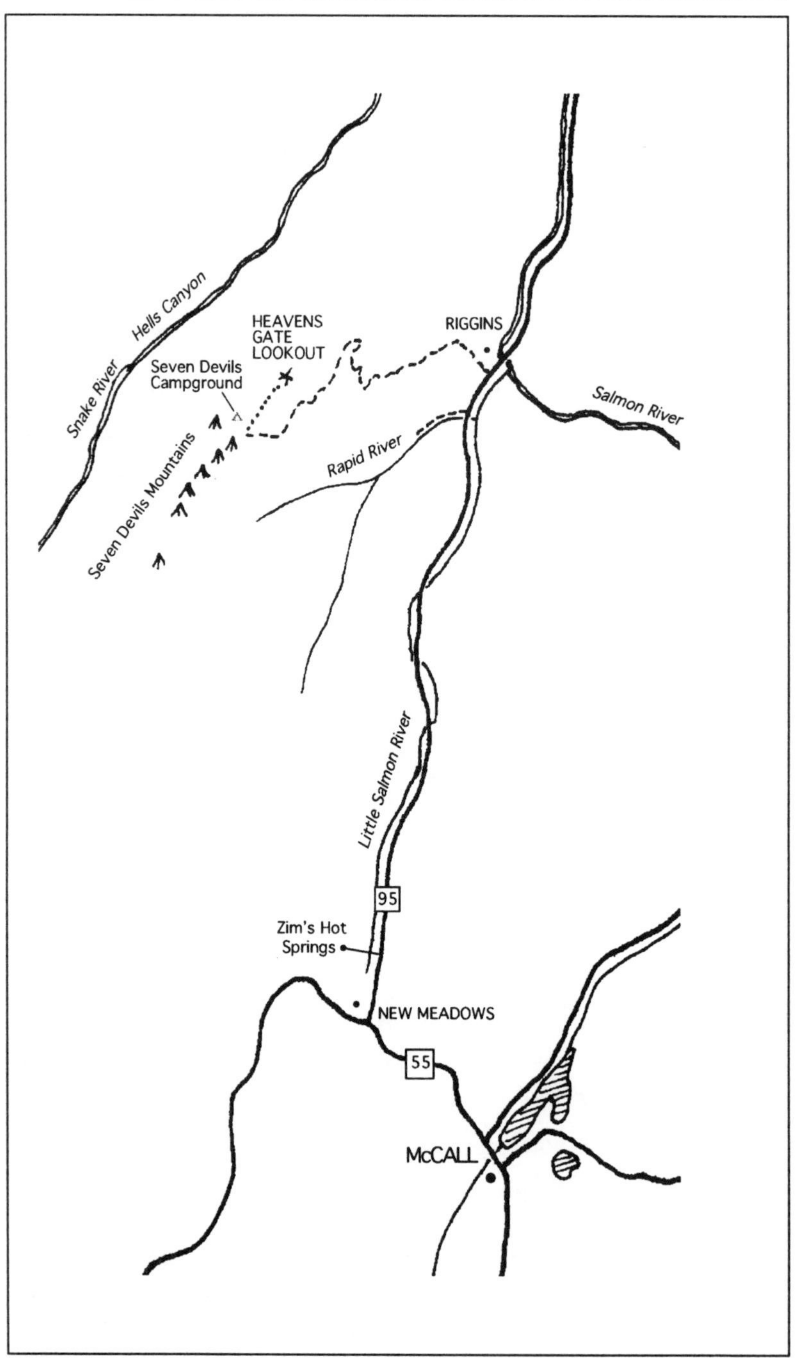
Hells Canyon
Snake River
Seven Devils
Campground
HEAVENS
GATE
LOOKOUT
RIGGINS
Salmon River
Seven Devils Mountains
Rapid River
Little Salmon River
95
Zim's Hot
Springs
NEW MEADOWS
55
McCALL

Seven Devils

Description

No other view is as breathtaking as that from Heavens Gate Lookout at the end of the Seven Devils Road. From here, you have a great look not only of the Seven Devils Mountains but also of Hells Canyon, the deepest river gorge in North America.

Distance/Direction/Conditions

The Seven Devils and Heavens Gate Lookout are part of the Hells Canyon Recreation and Wilderness Area located sixty-three miles northwest of McCall. Pavement covers the first forty-four miles of the road, followed by eleven miles of improved dirt road. The last five miles are rough and narrow. While a four-wheel drive isn't necessary, your car should have good clearance and good suspension. This road is not suitable for cars with low clearance, recreational vehicles, or vehicles pulling camping trailers.

Best Time to Travel

The road is open from early July to mid-October, depending on snow fall. Heavy rains may also make the road impassable. Road reports are available from the Hells Canyon Recreation Area office, located just south of Riggins. You should call to find the latest road conditions.

Facilities

Pit toilets are available at the end of the road.

Camping

A small Forest Service campground affords visitors a majestic view of the Seven Devils. Located on the edge of Seven Devil's Lake it features picnic tables, fire rings, and pit toilets.

On the Way

New Meadows–last chance for gas

Zim's Hot Springs–Located a few miles north of New Meadows on Highway 95, Zim's would be a great place to stop on the way home. The resort boasts two pools, one for swimming, the other for soaking. The swimming pool is maintained at a refreshing ninety-three degrees while the soaking pool is kept at 103F. Snacks and drinks are also available.

Sheep Creek Rest area–Mile 38

Pottenger's Mercantile–Located just a few miles south of the Seven Devil's road, Pottenger's is a good place to grab a snack, a cold drink, and the latest road information.

Caution

While the first forty miles to Seven Devils are easy traveling, the last twenty are not for the cowardly. The road is narrow, especially the last four miles, and you must be on constant lookout for other cars. Also, Seven Devils is a popular place for horsemen, and trucks pulling large stock trailers are a common occurrence. Finally, what goes up, must come down. This steep road is not recommended for vehicles with automatic transmissions unless they are equipped with low gear settings.

Getting There

From the northwest end of McCall, head north on Highway 55, eleven miles to New Meadows. At New Meadows, head north on Highway 95. At Mile 44, the Seven Devils Road will take off on your left and head west. Take this dirt road and follow the signs. Side roads will appear from time to time, but stay on the main road. It should be well-marked. At Mile 55.5, the road forks. Take the upper fork, to the right. The road now becomes extremely rough. Follow this for another four miles, until you reach Windy Saddle. At Windy Saddle, you will find picnic tables and public restrooms. From here, you can head west, one-half mile to Seven Devils Lake or follow the road north two more miles to Heavens Gate Lookout.

Miscellaneous

Heavens Gate lookout sits at an elevation of 8,429 feet; at that elevation even the warmest Idaho days are a bit cool. Bring a sweater or light jacket. Also pack sunscreen. At high elevations, the sun's rays are more intense and can cause a quick burn before you know it.

The Seven Devils Mountains from Heavens Gate Lookout

History

Seven Devils is the steepest mountain range in Idaho, rising 7,593 feet above Riggins in a span of just fifteen miles. On its precipitous west side, it plunges 8,043 feet to the Snake River, creating Hells Canyon, the deepest river gorge in North America.

As with all natural landmarks, stories vary as to how the Seven Devils were named. Two Indian legends survive. One states that the mountains were named by a young Indian who became lost. Frightened and delirious, he was surprised by the devil. When he ran, he encountered six more devils. When he finally found his way back to his tribe, he told the story of the seven devils, and thus the legend was born. The Nez Perce Indians added to the myth with the creation of Hells Canyon. They believe their clever ancestor, Coyote, dug Hells Canyon to protect their Wallowa homeland, which lies to the west, from the Seven Devils.

A more recent version of the nomenclature comes from Hudson Bay Company's trappers who visited the area in the early 1800s.

They claimed the high, forbidding peaks were the work of the devil.

The Seven Devils peaks lie in a semicircle with He Devil the tallest at 9,393 feet. She Devil, The Ogre, and The Goblin make a cluster southwest of He Devil. Then to the south stand Mt. Belial, Devils Throne and Twin Imps. Other high peaks lie outside of the group. Devils Tooth lies directly north and Tower of Babel sits to the northwest. At 9,268 feet, the Tower of Babel is equally as impressive.

The Seven Devils are composed of a complicated mix of rocks, from sedimentary to igneous, created by block faulting, which lifted the mountains high above the plains. At the same time, the Snake River to the west cut a deep and wide canyon; to the east the Salmon River with its wild waters cut a steep and narrow gorge. The result is a three mile wide upland between the two rivers which is home to the Seven Devils.

In addition to the mountains, the Seven Devils area is home to over twenty high mountain lakes, carved out by glaciers, and is a popular destination for hikers and backpackers exploring this rugged wilderness. The area is part of the 650,000 acre Hells Canyon National Recreation Area, established in 1975 and includes the Hells Canyon Wilderness, of which the Seven Devils are a part. Hikers can find 208 miles of trail leading to the high alpine lakes and forests of the Seven Devils.

Windy Saddle is one of two main trailheads leading into the wilderness area. Trails 124 and 101 take off from the saddle and offer great hiking to Basin, Sheep, Baldy and Cannon Lakes.These trails offer some of the best hiking in Central Idaho.

Even if you do not hike, you can still experience the magnificence of the Seven Devils by taking this drive. You can stop at Devils Lake Campground and enjoy lunch at the lake's edge, within shouting distance of the peaks. At the end of the road, a short walk (400 yards) to Heavens Gate Lookout is well-worth the effort. From the lookout, you get a bird's-eye view of four states, Hells Canyon, the Salmon River Canyon, and the Seven Devils. The vista can occupy you for hours.

For More Information

Hells Canyon National Recreation Area
P.O. Box 832
Riggins, Idaho 83549
(208) 628-3916
Office Hours: 8 a.m. to 5 p.m. MST
Maps and brochures are available

Cuprum/Bear

Description

Today Bear and Cuprum are quiet recreation and summer home areas, but in the late 1800s, the region was alive with mining activity. Remnants of these earlier times are evident on many of the backroads in the area.

Distance/Direction/Conditions

Bear and Cuprum are located west of McCall and on the south end of the Seven Devils Mountains. Round trip distance is 155 miles, with sixty-four paved miles to Bear. From there, a well-maintained, improved dirt road leads seven miles to Cuprum. The loop from Cuprum back to Bear, through the old mining country, is narrow, rough, and rugged. It is suitable for SUVs or vehicles with high clearance, but should not be attempted unless you have faith in your vehicle and your driving skills. Also, avoid traveling the loop in the spring when the road can be muddy and slick.

Best Time to Travel

Weekend travel in Central Idaho means busy highways and back roads. To avoid this, travel to Bear and Cuprum during the week, when you should have the area to explore in peace and quiet.

Facilities

None

Camping

The Forest Service has two established campgrounds near Bear. Lafferty Campground, fifty-seven miles into the trip, features camp sites, fire rings, picnic tables, and pit toilets. Water is also available at the site, which was renovated in 2003.

Five miles north of Bear is Huckleberry Campground, another Forest Service facility. The campground is open June through November and has eight campsites, including those suitable for camp trailers. Potable water is also available.

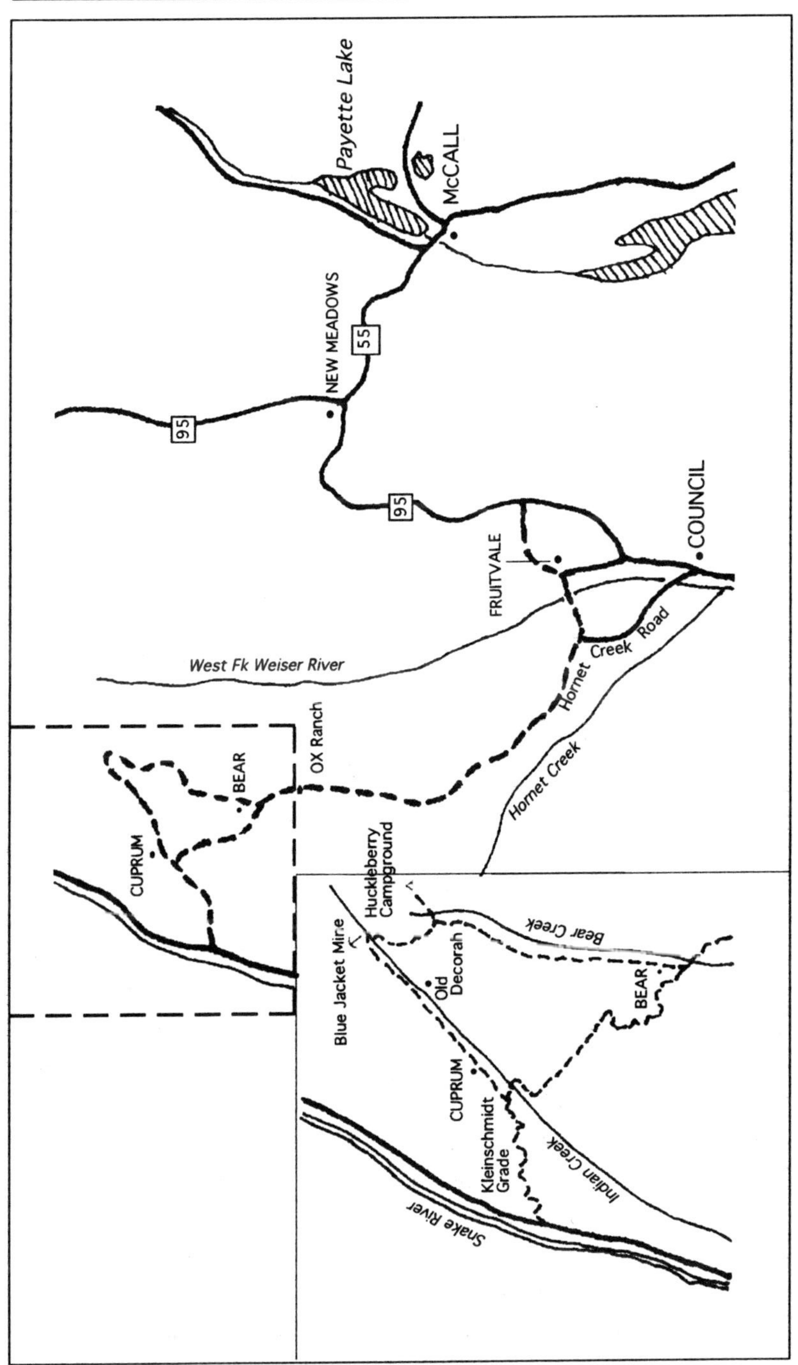

Payette Lake
McCALL
NEW MEADOWS
55
95
95
COUNCIL
FRUITVALE
West Fk Weiser River
Hornet Creek Road
Hornet Creek
OX Ranch
BEAR
CUPRUM
Huckleberry Campground
Bear Creek
Blue Jacket Mine
Old Decorah
BEAR
CUPRUM
Kleinschmidt Grade
Indian Creek
Snake River

On the Way

Tamarack Mill

Council, the county seat of Adams of County, features convenience stores and gas stations.

Eagle Cap Mountains–Mile 58 to the west, part of the Wallowa Range in Oregon

Huntley Barn–A local landmark located 1.5 miles south of Cuprum, the barn was completed in 1910. It is three stories high and measures 40 by 100 feet. It is one of the few three-story barns in the state still standing. It is also known as the Speropulos Barn, after a Greek sheepherder who bought the place in 1929.

Caution

The canyon highway from McCall to Council is narrow and winding. It can also be slick when wet. Once past Council, you will be passing through open range and the OX ranch. Be on the lookout for cattle, anytime and anywhere. Finally, the back-country route from Cuprum to Bear through the old mining country is extremely rough and steep, certainly a "road less traveled." If you are an explorer, the trip is worth it, but if you are just out for a comfortable day drive, you may want to retrace your route to Bear.

Getting There

From the northwest end of McCall, take Highway 55, eleven miles to New Meadows. Once in New Meadows, head twenty-four miles south on Highway 95 to Council. As you enter Council, Highway 95 will make a ninety-degree turn to the right. Make this turn. A few blocks later, Highway 95 will turn sharp to the left, but you will go straight on to Hornet Creek Road, also known as the Council/Cuprum Road.

From Council, the road leads eleven miles through a picturesque valley before heading into higher country. A new highway, completed in 2002, will take you past Hornet Creek and wander through varying terrain until Mile 58. Here the road will reach the boundaries of the OX Ranch, located on one of the many plains high above the Snake River. Follow the road as it travels through the ranch land. Immediately after leaving the ranch, you will come to an intersection. Turn left on the Council/Cuprum road and drive for seven miles. Here you will see the Speropulos barn, a well-known landmark, and arrive at an intersection. A left turn will lead to the Kleinschmidt grade and the Snake River; a right turn will take you 1.5 miles to Cuprum.

Cuprum's only street is one lane wide, with cabins on either side of the road. If you are adventurous and have a vehicle with high clearance, continue through Cuprum following FS Road 105.

At Mile 74, a road takes off to the east toward Horse Mountain Lookout and a scenic overlook of Hells Canyon. It is worth the view, but it is a bumpy drive. As you continue on FS 105, you will pass the old townsite of Decorah and the remains of the Bluejacket Mine. At Mile 80, a historical marker will identify the site of Landore. From here, you will begin a sharp descent. After two miles, you will reach an intersection. A left turn will take you to the Huckleberry Campground; turn right to Bear. Continue through Bear until you reach the Council/Cuprum road and begin your return trip home.

Miscellaneous Information

This is a long drive into a sparsely populated area. While the road to Bear and Cuprum is in good shape, the back-country loop that connects the two requires a good vehicle and confident driving skills. Plan to take your time and make a day of it. The area offers interesting history, but you have to be willing to explore. This is also one trip where a map of the Payette National Forest could come in handy.

History

No other area in Idaho produced as much promise and disappointment as the mining areas located north of Cuprum and Bear. Located on the southern edge of the forbidding Seven Devils, the large deposits of copper made dreamers of all who saw them, but rugged terrain, unscrupulous businessmen, and bad judgment all led to dreams that could not come true.

In 1862, Levi Allen led a group of men from Lewiston to explore the Snake and Salmon Rivers for possible navigation routes. They also planned to do a little prospecting. Their travels took them to Pittsburg Landing, up the steep slopes of the Snake River Canyon, and down into the Little Salmon River drainage. They made their way to Payette Lake and followed the Payette River to Horseshoe Bend before deciding to return to Pittsburg Landing. Looking for a different route home, Allen led the men into the southern end of the Seven Devils where the party discovered an outcropping of bright blue rock, which they reported as 550 feet long and eight feet wide. It turned out to be a rich copper strike. In July of 1862, Allen filed a mining claim for the site and called it the Peacock Lode because of its color.

Allen waited until 1877 to promote the mine. That year, he traveled to Montana looking for investors, which he found. He also established two other mines, the Helena and White Monument. After attracting the attention of Helena businessmen, including Albert Kleinschmidt, Allen sold the remaining interests in his claims.

Kleinschmidt was an entrepreneur with an adventurous spirit who saw the potential of the Seven Devils. He bought shares in the Peacock, Helena, and White Monument mines; he also purchased the Blue Jacket, Queen, and Alaska mines. However, he was well aware of the area's major weakness–inaccessibility. Because of this, he developed a plan that would link his mines to Ballard's Ferry on the Snake River. From there he was sure his ore could be transported by boat to the railroad lines near Weiser.

In May of 1890, work began on what is now known as the Kleinschmidt Grade. An engineering marvel, the road ran twenty miles from the Helena mine to the Snake River, at a cost of $1,000 per mile. In addition, Kleinschmidt invested in a steamship, the *Norma.* His goal was to pack the ore to the steamship and then have the steamship carry the ore to the nearest railroad lines where it could then be transported for processing.

Crews finished the road in July 1891, but Kleinschmidt's plan was a failure. The jagged rocks and unpredictable rapids of the Snake were too much for the *Norma.* Badly damaged in her trial run down the river, the *Norma* failed to carry any ore from the mines.

Following the failure, mining activity slowed. Hopes rested on the coming of the railroad to the area. Speculation and scams followed over the next forty years, and more money was lost than was ever made. Still, miners and investors continued to see the value of the area. Freighters took over the job of hauling the ore to distant smelters and towns sprung up overnight.

Helena, originally called the Town of Seven Devils, was the first recognized town in the area with a post office established in 1890. It was located near the Peacock and Helena mines, seven miles northeast of present Cuprum. Eventually it featured a brewery, two sawmills, two assay offices, three general stores, and six saloons. The establishments were supported by Helena's 100 residents.

Bear was supposedly named for the abundance of black bear found by the first settlers in the area. It was a stopover for freighters hauling ore from the Alaska and Blue Jacket mines by way of Council to Weiser. The town, founded by John Warner, had a post office as early as 1892.

Cuprum followed, the result of another road project by Albert Kleinschmidt. After the failure of the river route, Kleinschmidt continued to look for alternative methods to transport his ore. The result was a new road that lead from the Kleinschmidt road to Bear. The roads intersected in a meadow, and immediately a general store sprang up at the site. That was followed by a sawmill and a hotel. In 1897, the town of Cuprum was established. Eventually the community boasted all the services of a small town, including a livery stable, drug store, hospital, and a newspaper, the *Standard.*

No town in the area could live up to the prosperity of Landore, whose rise spelled the demise of Cuprum. With the road from Bear to Landore shorter and easier than that to Cuprum, freighters adapted their routes to the new town. Platted and sold in lots to miners and merchants alike, Landore boasted a population of 1,000 during its boom in the early 1900s. A daily stage ran from Landore to Council and the community established the first school in the area. Landore's fortunes were further enhanced with the construction of a smelter in 1903. At its peak, Landore featured a bank, a law office, two blacksmith shops, and three saloons.

By far the most interesting town in the area was Decorah, founded in 1898, just four miles northeast of Cuprum. The founder of Decorah had just one purpose in mind: serve the miners of the area with whatever they might need: saloon, hotel, barber shop and three whore-houses, all located on Main Street. Decorah's notoriety was short lived, however. When mining prospects dimmed in 1902 because of continued transportation problems, Decorah ceased to exist.

The other towns soon followed Decorah to extinction. Of all the communities, only Bear and Cuprum survive, home to a few full-time and many part-time residents. Ruins and historical markers detail the existence of Helena, Decorah and Landore. What Idaho's state mine inspector J.H. Czizek promised in 1899 fell far short: "The Seven Devils District has some of the best copper prospects in the world. It is destined at no distant day to rival Butte, Montana, in wealth and productiveness of its copper mine." In spite of the best efforts of man, the mountains refused to yield up their copper; now the area is a beautiful, historical footnote in Idaho's past.

For More Information

Payette National Forest
Council Ranger District
500 E. Whitley
Council, Idaho 83612
(208) 253-0100

A Wild Cowboy
by Heidi Bigler Cole

French Creek

Description

The French Creek road takes you on a magnificent tour into Salmon River Country. This drive is not for the faint of heart, but definitely worth the time and effort.

Distance/Direction/Conditions

The French Creek route makes a 118 mile loop through the heart of central Idaho, northwest of McCall. The journey will take you on paved highways, improved gravel roads, and several miles of one-lane dirt road.

Best time to travel

The road is open late May to early October, depending on the snow season. Avoid weekends if possible, as the Salmon River is a popular attraction for weekend getaways. This is also a busy time for river outfitters. If you go in July and August, temperatures hover in the high 90's, so take plenty of water.

Facilities

None are available until you reach Riggins, seventy-four miles into the trip. There you will find restaurants, motels, convenience stores, and gas stations.

Camping

On the first half of the trip, good campsites can be found at Upper Payette Lake and the Burgdorf Campground. Once you have reached the Salmon River, camping is available at Wind River, Spring Bar, and Allison Creek. All are Forest Service campgrounds with water, picnic tables, and pit toilets.

On the Way

Fisher Creek is approximately ten miles north of McCall. In September, Fisher Creek is teeming with bright red Kokanee salmon, which travel up the river to spawn.

Burgdorf–natural hot springs open to the public (see page 68)

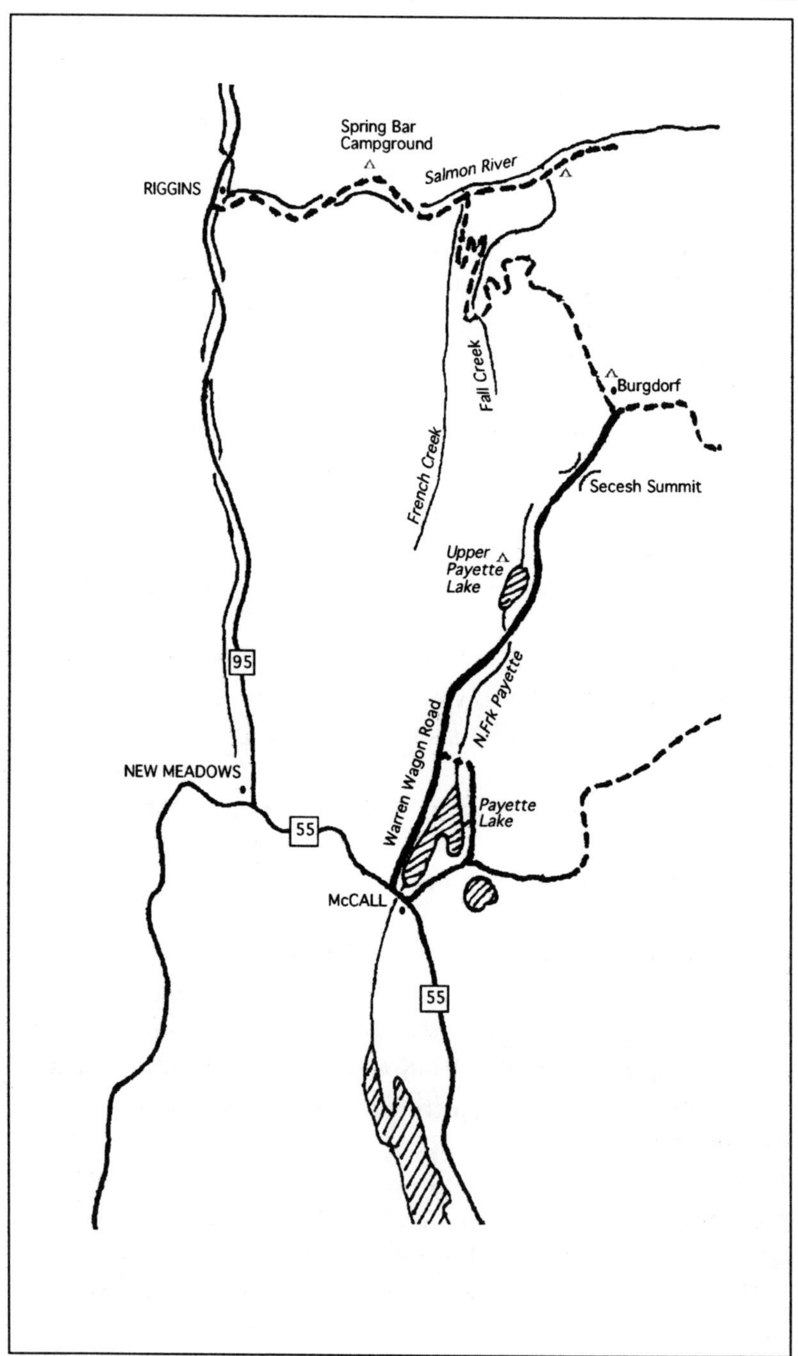
Spring Bar
Campground
Salmon River
RIGGINS
Fall Creek
Burgdorf
French Creek
Secesh Summit
Upper
Payette
Lake
95
N.Frk Payette
Warren Wagon Road
NEW MEADOWS
Payette
Lake
55
McCALL
55

French Creek Grade–This man-made marvel takes you to the Salmon River.

The Crevice–One of the narrowest points on the Salmon River, a one-lane suspended bridge spans the river here.

Spring Bar Campground, Allison Creek Campground, numerous sandy beaches–All are suitable for picnics. Both Spring Bar and Allison Creek offer picnic tables with shade.

Lodge at Riggins Hot Springs–This private, rustic resort features fine food and a natural hot springs pool. Reservations are required.

Riggins–Restaurants, convenience stores, and gas stations are available.

Rapid River Fish Hatchery–south of Riggins (see page 20)

Zim's Hot Springs–A few miles north of New Meadows, Zim's would be a great place to stop on the way home. For a fee, families can enjoy the two naturally-heated pools, one for swimming, one for soaking.

Getting There

From the northwest end of McCall, take Warren Wagon Road north towards Warren. Follow the shore of Payette Lake and then the North Fork of the Payette River to its beginnings at Upper Payette Lake. The route will take you over Secesh Summit and then down to the headwaters of the Secesh River at Lake Creek.

Immediately following Lake Creek Bridge, at Mile 28, turn left (north) on Forest Road 246. You will be on an improved gravel road. After a little over one mile, you will pass Burgdorf. Continue on this road, heading north and northwest, to t
Salmon River. The road will take you through varied terra
from full, green forests with fast rushing streams, to the m
arid slopes of Salmon River country. Drive carefully as you v
your way down the French Creek grade, also known as
Fingers" because of its appearance on a map.

At approximately Mile 55, you will reach the Salmo
Turn left (west) and follow the river. You will be on a
dirt road which will eventually turn to pavement. F

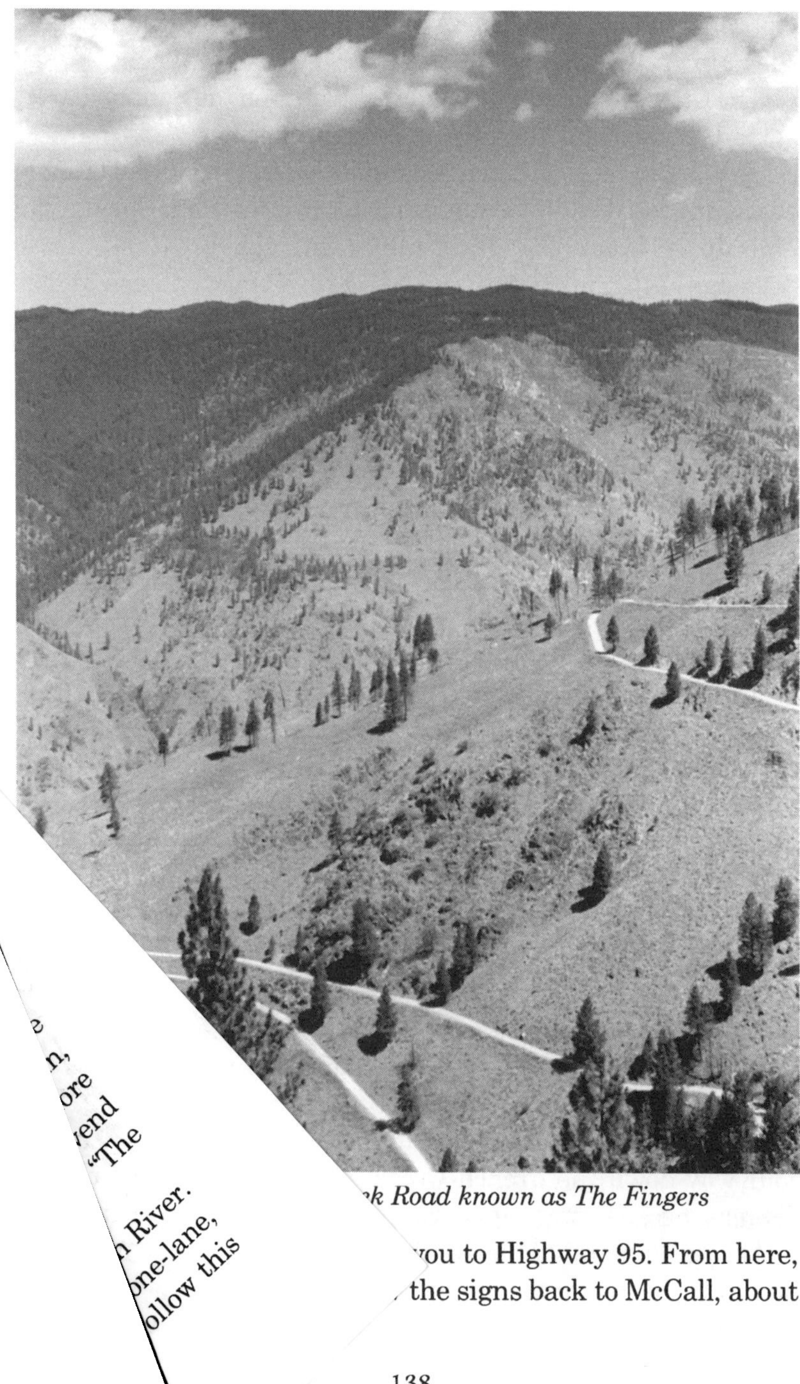

...k Road known as The Fingers

...you to Highway 95. From here, ... the signs back to McCall, about

Caution

This route is not suitable for recreational vehicles or vehicles pulling trailers. Avoid this route after heavy rains, as portions of the dirt road can be slick if water is on the roadway. Finally, portions of the road following the Salmon River are winding and extremely narrow. Keep an eye peeled for approaching cars and always be prepared to use the pull-outs.

This road is in Idaho's backcountry. Make sure you have water, plenty of gas, a spare tire, and a vehicle you can count on.

Miscellaneous

If you want a side trip, follow the road east when you arrive at the Salmon River. The road will take you six more miles to the Wind River Pack Bridge, Vinegar Creek Boat Ramp, and the end of the road. You will find several vantage points from which to watch boaters negotiate some Class III rapids.

History

French Creek roars as it makes its way to the Salmon River. It sounds the same today as it did over 100 years ago when the first miners traveled this route in search of their fortunes.

Gold was discovered in the hills north of French Creek in 1861, giving birth to the town of Florence. This was followed by a gold strike in Warren, to the southeast, in 1862. In the forty years following, miners and freighters needed a route that would take them to the various mining communities and the more established Idaho towns. The French Creek Trail became that route.

French Creek, which derives its name from the French miners who settled there, was the Salmon River crossing point for miners and freighters on the French Creek Trail. Over the years various types of ferries and crossings were established here. The first ferry was operated by Montgomery Fullerton who moved to the site in 1862. In November 1863, he sold the ferry boat, a cabin, and one half of the French Creek Trail to William Knott. Knott paid seven hundred dollars in potatoes, at twenty cents per pound, for the property.

Shortly thereafter, Knott was granted a ferry franchise by

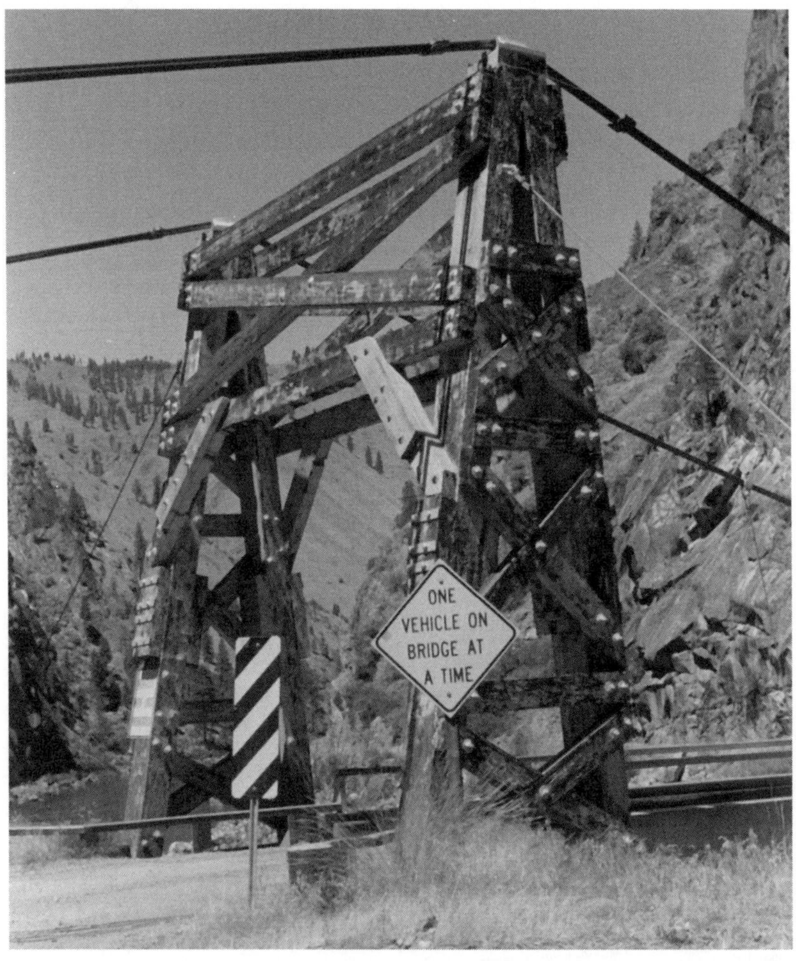

A one-lane bridge over the Salmon River

the Idaho Territorial Legislature. He maintained the ferry for the next three years, before selling it to Frank Shissler for $2500 in June 1865.

The ferry operated for the next twenty-five years. Then, in 1889, the Idaho Territorial Legislature allocated $32,240 to build a road, complete with a bridge, from Mt. Idaho, near Grangeville to Meadows Valley, west of McCall. The road, similar to what exists today, joined the existing road to Meadows Valley at Wagon Bay on Payette Lake, followed north along the lake shore, crossed Secesh Summit, passed Burgdorf, and then descended to the Salmon River at French Creek, where a bridge was to be built. From there, the road led to Florence and to Mt. Idaho, near present Grangeville.

Construction on the road began that year, but the bridge proved to be the biggest obstacle. Steel supports designated for the Salmon River bridge somehow ended up in Spokane, Washington; the ones that arrived for the Salmon River were fifty feet short. Eventually, the bridge was completed and the first traffic crossed in 1892. The route was a godsend to freighters. The Edmunson Cabin built in 1900 (located forty-three miles into the trip) was a major freight stop.

The route was designated an Idaho State Highway in the spring of 1901. The need for the road diminished, however, as the mining areas of Florence and Warren began to fade. When the bridge blew down in a storm in November of that year, the state did not rebuild.

The road and the area saw little development until the 1930s with the arrival of the Civilian Conservation Corps. The men were put to work building the Salmon River Road, which follows the Salmon River from French Creek to Riggins. They built the present French Creek Grade and were responsible for the suspension bridge located a few miles west of French Creek, at an area known as the "The Crevice," a very narrow stretch of the river. In 1939, the CCC constructed a tram at French Creek which once again allowed people to cross the river and use the trail to Florence. The Forest Service closed the tram in 1995 deeming it a danger to the public. It has since been dismantled.

The Secesh and French Creek drainages have been ravaged the past twenty-five years by forest fires. In the summer of 2000, a fire raged west of Burgdorf and eventually made its way to the Salmon River. Its damage can be seen on some of the hills to the west as you drive from Burgdorf to the river. Secesh Summit was torched in September 1994, when three major fires merged, creating a fire cloud seen for miles around. French Creek burned in 1984, and the road was kept open the following the winter to salvage the trees for local lumber mills. While signs of this fire are still visible, in the past few years the forest here has made a remarkable comeback.

Today, the French Creek and Salmon River Roads lead to recreation. Gone are the miners and freighters who worked the claims and hauled supplies. In their place are boaters and hikers, anglers and hunters. While their purposes are now very different, the ruggedness and beauty of the area remain.

For Further Information

Payette National Forest
McCall Ranger District
102 W. Lake Street
McCall, Idaho 83638
(208) 634-0400

Idaho County Road Department
(208) 628-3608

Idaho County Sheriff
(208) 983-1100

Be Prepared

Cell Phone	Full Tank of Gas	Spare Tire
Flares/Matches	Tow Rope	Jumper Cables
Extra Car Key	Sun Screen	Insect Repellent
Water	Blanket	Food
Shovel	Bucket	Ax

Driving the back roads around McCall is not a risky proposition, but it is prudent always to be prepared for whatever may come your way. Common sense, of course, is your best weapon against adversity, but even that sometimes can fail. Midsummer snow and wind storms, an animal darting quickly across your path, or even a sharp rock in the road can cause problems. But if you are prepared, you can turn these possible disasters into small inconveniences.

Central Idaho's mountains can raise havoc with cell phone reception; still, you should carry one with you on all of your travels. You might just be on top of a summit or in a high valley when you need it. In that case, help is just a phone call away.

Because the reception is hit and miss, however, you should be prepared in other ways. Always leave town with a full tank of gas. Most of these back-country destinations do not have gasoline available for you to buy. If you are running the air conditioner in your vehicle, you may use more gas than you anticipate and may find yourself running on fumes. A full tank of gas will ensure that you arrive at your destination and return home without having to call for help.

Another item you should have in your car is a tow rope. One can hope you will never be in a position where you have to be pulled out of a ditch, but you should be prepared. The rope also comes in handy to pull others out of trouble as well. More importantly, a tow rope can be used to pull downed limbs and small trees out of the roadway, a common occurrence in Central Idaho's mountains, especially after high winds. Along with the tow rope, you should carry flares. Both will come in handy in case of an accident.

A spare tire, properly inflated, is essential on these trips, as is a jack and the knowledge of how to change a tire. Jumper cables are also a good idea, in the event your battery decides to desert you. A hide-a-key, somewhere on the outside of your vehicle, would also be a good investment. Automatic door locks, precocious children, and simple forgetfulness could lead to a locked car; waiting for a locksmith in Idaho's back country can spoil even the best day.

As for noncar items, consider a shovel and a bucket and maybe even a small hatchet or ax. They may come in handy during the summer fire season, and if you stop to build a campfire in one of the Forest Service campgrounds, they are required equipment. Of course, to build a fire, you will need matches. You will also need matches to light your flares in the case of an accident.

You also need to consider some emergency gear for yourself. Never leave home without water. While Idaho's streams and rivers look clean, they carry various micro-organisms, including giardia, which make the water unfit to drink. While many of the Forest Service campgrounds have spigots and pumps, sometimes they do not work, so you cannot entirely depend on them. Thus, carrying your own water is the only sure way to stay hydrated. Always throw in a blanket and an extra coat. In the event of an accident or car trouble, some way to keep warm will be important, as nights in Idaho's mountains, even in the middle of summer, can dip to below freezing. Sunscreen and mosquito repellent are also essential items. At higher elevations, the sun's rays are particularly intense, even if the temperature is cool. As for the mosquitoes, they can be vicious, especially in late June and early July. Finally, always take a snack with you. If you should find yourself stuck overnight in your car, the morning will seem a bit brighter if you can treat yourself to a little food.

No activity is without risks, but taking a few precautions and using common sense can make any drive in Idaho's heartland an enjoyable experience.

Emergency Contacts

Although you may plan your back-country drive carefully, you never know when you might need some extra help. While cell phones do not always work in Central Idaho's mountains, many of the back country communities have telephone service. If you have a problem, do not hesitate to stop at a home or business and ask if a phone is available. Most residents of central Idaho are always willing to lend a hand.

Locksmiths

May Hardware
McCall, Idaho
(208) 634-7665

Miller Hardware
Grangeville, Idaho
(208) 983-0380

Cross Country Lock and Key
Council, Idaho
(208) 253-0001

Towing

AAA Towing
McCall
(208) 634-5342

Collins Body and Paint
McCall
(208) 634-8400

McCall Tire and Auto
McCall
(208) 634-2539

ABT Towing
New Meadows
(208) 634-3808

Towing (continued)

Mountain Towing
Cascade
(208) 382-7268

Clear Creek Station
Cascade
(208) 382-3166

C & B Towing
Grangeville
(208) 983-2378

Dale's Rescue Towing
Grangeville
(208) 983-0671

Kirt's Repair
Council
(208) 253-6860

Law Enforcement

Valley County Dispatch
Cascade
(208) 382-5160

Idaho County
Riggins and Whitebird
(208) 983-1100

Adams County
Council
(208) 253-4227

Idaho State Police
(208) 334-2900

For emergencies
911

Road Conditions

Idaho County
Riggins
(208) 628-3608

Valley County
Cascade
(208) 382-7195

Payette National Forest
Council District
(208) 253-0100

Krassel District
(208) 634-0600

McCall District
(208) 634-0409

Road reports for the Payette National Forest can also be found at www.fs.fed.us/r4/payette/main.html

McCall Attractions

While the area around McCall makes for great scenic drives, you can find plenty of other activities to keep you busy. From local points of interest to day trips on the Salmon River, Central Idaho will provide you with plenty of excursions to make your stay in McCall memorable.

Please keep in mind, however, that in McCall and the surrounding areas, businesses open and close depending on the season and the economy. The following list of recreational sites and providers is as accurate as possible but is subject to change. If you plan to stop at an establishment or use the services of an outfitter, you should always call ahead.

Sites of Local Interest

Ponderosa State Park

Located at the end of Davis Street on the shores of Payette Lake, Ponderosa Park features two swimming beaches, miles of hiking and biking trails, scenic overlooks, and a boat ramp. Groups can reserve a covered picnic area for large gatherings. Call (208) 634-2164 for information.

McCall Smoke Jumper Base

Smoke jumpers are the Forest Service's first line of defense against wildfires, and the McCall Jumper Base is home to seventy of this elite corps of fire fighters. The jumpers were first brought to McCall in 1943. Since then their operation has expanded, culminating in the construction of a modern jumper base, completed in 1988. Located at 605 S. Mission, the facility provides excellent guided tours throughout the summer. Call (208) 634-0390 for tour times and information.

Central Idaho Cultural Center

Located just off Highway 55 at 1001 State Street, the Cultural Center is the home of various exhibits that document the history of the timber industry in Central Idaho. The center is housed at the original site of the Southern Idaho Timber Protective Association, and the building, constructed by the Civilian Conservation Corps, is part of the National Register of Historic Places. Call (208) 634-4497 for hours and information.

McCall Fish Hatchery

Located at 300 Mather Road on the banks of the North Fork of the Payette River, the McCall Fish Hatchery's charge is to restore the Chinook salmon runs on the South Fork of the Salmon River. The hatchery is open 8 a.m. to 5 p.m., seven days a week for self-guided tours. You can also ask for more information by calling (208) 634-2690.

Golf Courses

McCall Public Golf Course
Reedy Lane
twenty-seven holes
(208) 634-7200

Meadow Creek Golf Course
three miles north of New Meadows
eighteen holes
(208) 347-2555

Cascade Public Golf Course
on the shores of Cascade Lake
nine holes
(208) 387-4835

Trail Rides

Heaven's Gate Outfitters
2064 E. Side Drive
McCall, Idaho
(208) 634-5999

Ya-Hoo Corrals
2280 Warren Wagon Road
McCall, Idaho
(208) 634-3360

Big Foot Outfitters
Riggins, Idaho
(208) 628-3539 or 888-570-2666

Big Creek Lodge & Outfitters
Big Creek, Idaho
888-848-0011

Northwest Voyageurs
Lucille, Idaho
(208) 628-3021

Salmon River Challenge
Riggins, Idaho
(208) 628-3264 or 800-732-8574

Unique Dining Experiences

Ya-Hoo Corral
Wagon Rides and Barbeques
McCall, Idaho
(208) 634-3360

Snowbank Outfitters

Wagon and Sleigh Ride Dinners
Western Style Cookouts
Highway 55 at Clear Creek
(208) 382-4872

Blue Moon Outfitters

Ski to your dinner in Ponderosa Park
McCall, Idaho
(208) 634-3111

Train Rides

Thunder Mountain Line

A unique experience for families is the Thunder Mountain Line train rides. Visitors have their choice of three routes, all following the Payette River. Rides begin in Cascade or Horseshoe Bend, with lunch and dinner service available on some routes.

Call for reservations, schedules, and fares.
877-432-7245 or (208) 793-4425

Rafting and Jet Boat Trips

The rivers around McCall provide plenty of activities for visitors, from rafting to jet boating to fishing. Following is a list of outfitters who provide a variety of services. You can find half-day and full-day trips on the Salmon, Payette, and Snake Rivers.

Salmon River Challenge

Riggins, Idaho
(208) 628-3264 or 800-732-8574

Erekson Outfitters
McCall, Idaho
(208) 634-4092

Brundage Mountain Adventures
McCall and Riggins, Idaho
(208) 628-4212 or 888-889-8320

Epley's Whitewater Adventures
McCall, Idaho
(208) 634-5173 or 800-233-1813

River Adventures
Riggins, Idaho
(208) 628-3952 or 800-524-9710

Canyon Cats
Riggins, Idaho
(208) 628-3772 or 888-628-3772

Exodus Wilderness Adventures
Riggins, Idaho
(208) 628-3484

Wapiti River Guides
Riggins, Idaho
(208) 628-3523 or 800-488-9872

The Last Resort Outfitters and Guides
New Meadows, Idaho
(208) 628-3029

Cascade Raft Company
Horseshoe Bend, Idaho
(208)793-2221 or 800-292-7238

Headwaters River Company
Banks, Idaho
(208)793-2348 or 800-800-7238

Red Woods Outfitter
Polluck, Idaho
(208) 628-3673

Northwest Voyageurs
Lucille, Idaho
(208) 628-3021

Holiday River Adventures
Grangeville, Idaho
(208) 983-1518 or 800-628-2565

R & R Outdoors, Inc
Pollock, Idaho
(208) 628-3034 or 800-574-1224

Natsoh Koos River Outfitters
Riggins, Idaho
(208) 628-3131 or 800-539-3963

Mackay Bar Corporation
Boise, Idaho
(208)344-9905 or 800-854-9904

Acknowledgments

I have always considered myself fortunate to live in Idaho; to be able to write about the area I love is an added bonus.

For the past year, I have traveled the highways and backroads around McCall to the areas I enjoy, documenting my travels so others may enjoy them too. My hope is that people who choose these routes and destinations will appreciate and respect them as much as I do.

Road trips are best when they are shared with good friends. For this project, I had several who were always more than willing to jump into the passenger's seat and put up with my driving, as well as my frequent picture stops. Among these were Marquita Blanton, Joan Babineau, Ellen McKinney, Amber Strickler, and Jim Rush. Others, like Bonnie and Patricia Todeschi, set up meetings with "friends of friends" so I could research some of the more obscure history of the area. Their interest in my work and their encouragement made this project more than enjoyable.

A guide book is useless without maps and pictures. Peter Preston came through with the maps, and Earl Brockman rescued my photos with his dark room wizardry. Guide books must also be readable; for that I thank my editor, Frances Ford, whom I consider a grammar goddess.

I must also thank my parents, who raised me in this great state and continually encourage me in all my endeavors.

Finally, a great deal of gratitude goes to Robert and Aletha Hill, who over the years have traveled the roads around McCall in everything from a Pontiac Bonneville to a Volkswagen Bug. Their adventurous spirits gave me the idea for this book.

Kathy Deinhardt Hill
2002

Bibliography

Boone, Lalia. *Idaho Place Names.* Moscow, Idaho: University of Idaho Press, 1988.

Brown, Jayne. *Where Finland's Part of Idaho.* Unpublished Manuscript. McCall Public Library, 1939.

Brown, Warren. *It's Fun to Remember.* McCall, Idaho: n.p., 1999.

Carrey, Johnny, Cort Conley, and Ace Barton. *Snake River of Hells Canyon.* Cambridge, Idaho: Backeddy Books, 1979.

Clark, Bob. *Scenic Driving Idaho.* Helena, Montana: Falcon Publishing, Inc. 1998.

Cole, Heidi Bigler. *A Wild Cowboy.* Cambridge, Idaho: Rocky Mountain Comfort Press, 1992.

Conley, Cort. *Idaho for the Curious.* Cambridge, Idaho: Backeddy Books, 1982.

Cox, Emma and Lafe Cox. *Idaho Mountains Our Home.* Yellow Pine, Idaho: V.O. Ranch Books, 1997.

Crawford, Kaitlin. *Early History of Brundage Mountain.* Unpublished Manuscript.

Elsensohn, Sister M. Alfreda. *Pioneer Days in Idaho County, Volume I.* Cottonwood, Idaho: Idaho Corporation of Benedictine Sisters, 1978.

Fisk, Dale. *Landmarks: A general history of the Council, Idaho area.* Boise: Writers Press, 2001.

Gibbs, Rafe. *Beckoning the Bold: The Story of the Dawning of Idaho.* Moscow, Idaho: University of Idaho Press, 1976.

Grote, Tom. "Brundage was built the old fashioned way." *Central Idaho Star News*: November, 1986.

———. "Mountain trek gave new life to Stibnite homes." *Central Idaho Star News*: March 13, 1985.

Idaho's Highway History, 1863-1975. Boise: Idaho Transportion Department, 1985.

Ingraham, Beverly. *Looking Back: Sketches of Early Days in Idaho's High Country*. N.p.: n.p., 1992.

———. "Moving Stibnite homes required patience, skill." *Central Idaho Star News*: April 12, 1989.

Knight, Ruth T. *Molly of the Mountains*. Unpublished Manuscript. McCall Public Library.

Knudson, Lucia. "Stibnite mine clean-up almost done." *Central Idaho Star News*: September 6, 2001.

Lindsay, Winifred. "Seven Devils." *Idaho Yesterdays*. 14/2:12-18.

Lopez, Tom. *Exploring Idaho's Mountains. A guide for Climbers, Scramblers, and Hikers*. Seattle: Mountaineer Books, 1990.

Manser, Eunice Clay and Murrielle McGafee Wilson. *Riggins on the Salmon River*. Weiser, Idaho: n.p., 1983.

Matthews, Gratia. *Once Upon a Time Cascade was Born*. Boise: Mountain States Press, 1988.

McDermott, John D. *Forlorn Hope*. Boise: Idaho State Hisorical Society, 1978.

Meyer, W. Le Roy. *Warm Lake Area History*. Unpublished Manuscript. 2001.

O'Reilly, Betty. *The Magic of McCall*. McCall, Idaho: Better Books, 1989.

Petersen, Duane. *Three 'R's' the Hard Way. One Room School Houses of Valley County.* Cascade, Idaho: D & D Books, 2000.

———. *83 Miles of Hell. The Stibnite Ore Haul.* Cascade, Idaho: D & D Books, 1999.

Preston, Peter. *An Outline of the Cultural History of the Frank Church River of No Return Wilderness.* McCall: Payette National Forest Heritage Program, 2001.

Reddy, Sheila D. *Wilderness of the Heart.* McCall: Payette National Forest Heritage Program, 1995.

———. *Reluctant Fortune: The Story of the Seven Devils.* McCall: Payette National Forest Heritage Program, 1996.

Sparling, Wayne. *Southern Idaho Ghost Towns.* Caldwell: Caxton Printers, 1996.

Sumner, Nancy G. *Yellow Pine, Idaho.* N.p.: n.p., 1986.

Waters, Susan K. *Exploring Magical McCall and More.* N.p.: n.p., 1998.

Wilfong, Cheryl. *Following the Nez Perce Trail.* Corvallis, Oregon: Oregon State University Press, 1990.

Williams, Bill E. "Timber Protection Agencey Turns 95." *Central Idaho Star News*: May 27, 1999.

About the Author

Kathy Deinhardt Hill lives in McCall with her husband Bob. Her favorite route is the South Fork Road, especially on her bicycle.

In addition to *On the Road*, Deinhardt Hill is author of *Spirits of the Salmon River*, which documents the lives of people buried on the Salmon River. It is available at retail establishments in McCall, major book stores, and Amazon.com.

To contact the author or purchase signed copies of *On the Road* or *Spirits of the Salmon River*, write the author at Big Mallard Books, 14068 Pioneer Road, McCall, Idaho 83638 or call (208) 634-1062.